**ᵂʸPLAY
HOUSE**

Scuffer
by Mark Catley

Director Alex Chisholm
Designer Emma Williams
Video & Sound Designer Mic Pool
Lighting Designer Malcolm Rippeth
Music Consultant George Rodosthenous
Casting Director Kay Magson
Deputy Stage Manager Kim Lewis

First performance at West Yorkshire Playhouse, Courtyard Theatre, Leeds
on 10 March 2006

The Company

(in order of appearance)

Danny Richard Glaves
Cathy Lorraine Bruce
Amy Hannah Storey
Jack William Ilkley
Cauldron Dominic Gately

Other parts played by members of the company

Outloud (post-show discussion): Wednesday 22 March

Signed Performance: Tuesday 28 March 7.45pm
Interpreted by Ann Marie Bracchi

Captioned Performance: Friday 31 March 7.45pm
Captioned by Pam Wells

Audio Described Performances: Saturday 18 March 2.30pm &
Thursday 23 March 7.45pm
Audio described by Lynn Ecroyd & Neil Scott

Please note that smoking or the use of cameras or recording equipment is not permitted. Please ensure that mobile phones, pagers and digital alarms are SWITCHED OFF before you enter the auditorium.

Production thanks
BewleysHotels.com
William Hill
Napoleon's Casinos
Holy Moley Entertainment

Cast

Lorraine Bruce *Cathy*

Trained at ALRA. Theatre credits include: *Get Ken Barlow* (Watford Palace Theatre); *Romeo and Juliet* (Hull Truck); *Man of the Moment* (York Theatre Royal); *Mail Order Bride* (Oldham Coliseum); *The Rise and Fall of Little Voice* (Theatre Royal Bury St Edmunds); *Saucy Jack and the Space Vixens* (various productions). Television credits include: *The Bill, Dalziel and Pascoe, Time Gentlemen Please, The 11th Hour* (a new series with Patrick Stewart), several appearances in *Holby City*. Film credits include: *Provoked, Dark Corners*.

Dominic Gately *Cauldron*

Trained at Guildford School of Acting. Theatre credits include: *Romeo and Juliet* (national tour); *Othello* (Nottingham Playhouse); *Time at Moghul Gardens* (BBC Northern Exposure, Bradford Festival); *Pillars of Society* (Rosemary Branch, Islington); *Hamlet* (Cannizaro Park, Wimbledon); *Basil, Meggie and the Most Beautiful Man in the World, Perfect Light* (Theatre Workshop, Sheffield); *Bricks* (Theatre in the Mill, Bradford); *Castaway Café* (NCPM Sheffield/Edinburgh Fringe); *Bartholomew Fair* (Guildford Castle). Film credits include: *Virus-2050* (SBU); *The Best a Man Can Get* (Hynd). Radio credits include: *The Loves of Echo* and *Narcissus* (Yellow Arches). Dominic is a member of Slung Low Theatre Company, one of the largest emerging artist projects in the country. Slung Low's *1139 Miles* premieres in West Yorkshire in August 2006.

Richard Glaves *Danny*

Trained at Guildhall School of Music and Drama. Theatre credits include: *The Tempest* (Liverpool Playhouse); *Journey's End* (Duke of York's/UK tour); *Candida* (Oxford Stage Company) for which he was nominated for the 2004 Ian Charleson Award; *Twelfth Night* (Shakespeare's Globe/US tour); *Richard II, Edward II* (Shakespeare's Globe); *Habitat* (Royal Exchange, Manchester); *The Accrington Pals* (Minerva, Chichester); *The Clandestine Marriage* (Watermill, Newbury); *Spike* (Nuffield, Southampton); *The Boy Who Left Home* (ATC, Lyric Hammersmith/UK tour); *A Midsummer Night's Dream* (Wild Thyme, Neuss Shakespeare Festival, Germany). Television credits include: *Richard II – Live at Shakespeare's Globe* (BBC 4).

William Ilkley *Jack*

Trained at Rose Bruford. Theatre credits include: productions at Bolton Octagon, Manchester Royal Exchange, Newcastle Playhouse, Birmingham Rep, Theatr Clwyd, Watford Palace, Harrogate Theatre, Derby Playhouse, Leicester Haymarket, York Theatre Royal, West Yorkshire Playhouse. *Up N Under, Bouncers, September in the Rain, Happy Jack, The New Office Party* (Hull Truck); *Salt of the Earth* (Edinburgh Festival/national tour/ Donmar Warehouse/RSC); *Twelfth Night* (Edinburgh Festival/national tour/Donmar Warehouse); *Up N Under* (West End); *Lucky Sods* (national tour); *Gym and Tonic* (national tour); *Bouncers* (21st anniversary national tour); *Unleashed* (national tours); *Bouncers* (National

Theatre/national tour); *Seasons in the Sun* (West Yorkshire Playhouse). Television credits include: *Harry's Game, Doctor Who, Howard's Way, All Creatures Great and Small, The Bill, Last of the Summer Wine, Heartbeat, Emmerdale, Pigeon Summer, The Ward, Coronation Street, Wing and a Prayer, Gold, Hetty Wainthrop Investigates, Casualty, Judge John Deed, Dalziel and Pascoe, Holby City, The Last Detective, EastEnders, Battlefield Britain, Doctors, Family Affairs, Breaking the Chains, Vincent, Class of 76, Blade Camp*. Film credits include: *Defrosting the Fridge, And Small Zones, The Fix, Shipwrecked, The Whipping Boy, Night of the Fox, Paper Marriage, Between Two Women, The Jealous God, Thunder Road*. William owns and runs the company Dramart Productions Ltd which specialises in running performance arts workshop courses for schools and colleges.

Hannah Storey *Amy*

Trained at Rose Bruford. Theatre credits include: *Be My Baby* (Salisbury Playhouse); *The Trestle at Pope Lick Creek* (Southwark Playhouse/ Manchester Royal Exchange studio); *What It Takes To Keep A Young Girl Alive* (The Script Factory); *Wish* (Oval House); *Rita, Sue & Bob Too* (West Yorkshire Playhouse). Television credits include: *Spooks, Red Cap, Innocents, Nicholas Nickleby, Doctors, Dalziel and Pascoe, Perfect World II, Inspector Linley, Cops, Jack and the Beanstalk, Holby City, Hunt for the Yorkshire Ripper, The Bill, London's Burning, Casualty*. Radio credits include: *Street & Lane, Keeping Ann Marie, Man with Travel Hairdryer*.

Creatives

Mark Catley *Writer*

Mark was born in Leeds. He studied Performing Arts at Park Lane College, Leeds and subsequently took a BA in Drama and Theatre Arts at Goldsmiths College, University of London. Theatre credits include: *Crap Dad, Sunbeam Terrace* (West Yorkshire Playhouse); *Barkin', Dice, Frankie & Johnny, Angel* (Blah Blah Blah); *Too Broke to Fix, The Grimp* (Angel Productions). Television credits include: *EastEnders, Holby City, Doctors, Casualty* (BBC). Radio credits include: *Car 5, Flutterby* (BBC Radio 4). Directing credits include: *Players* (West Yorkshire Playhouse); *We Love You Arthur* (Northern Firebrand); *Too Broke To Fix* (Angel Productions – for whom Mark is Artistic Director). Mark has worked extensively on the last four Northern Exposure seasons as director, writer and, occasionally, performer. He also runs the *So You Want To Be A Writer?* course at West Yorkshire Playhouse.

Alex Chisholm *Director*

Alex studied History at Oxford University. She spent a year studying with Ian McKellen, Cameron Macintosh Professor of Contemporary Theatre, before completing the Postgraduate Directing course at Drama Studio London. Alex was appointed Literary Manager at the West Yorkshire Playhouse in December 2001. For West Yorkshire Playhouse she has directed *Non-Contact Time* by Jodie Marshall, *Huddersfield* by Ugljesa Sajtinac, English version by Chris Thorpe and *Sunbeam Terrace* by Mark Catley. In January 2005 she was invited by Yugoslav Drama Theatre in Belgrade to direct the Serbian Premiere of Huddersfield. This production is still running in repertoire and has won eight national awards including best play and best production. Previously, she spent seven years as a freelance director, assistant director and workshop leader, working for companies including Birmingham Rep, Chichester Festival Theatre, Royal National Theatre, Red Shift and Paines Plough.

Emma Williams *Designer*

Most recent designs include: *Of Mice & Men* (Mind The Gap); *The Shoe* (Polka Theatre); *The Dice Project* (Blah Blah Blah); *The Magic Paintbrush, The Dutiful Daughter, Runaway Diamonds* (West Yorkshire Playhouse). Other design work includes: *Crap Dad, Sunbeam Terrace, The Elves and the Shoemakers, Two Tracks and Text Me, Huddersfield, Coming Around Again, Pinocchio, Broken Angel* (West Yorkshire Playhouse); *Stuck, Thin Skin, Unmade Beds, Antigore, Barkin, Grass, Ho Ho Ho* (Blah Blah Blah).

Mic Pool
Video and Sound Designer

In a 29-year career in theatre sound, Mic has been resident at the Lyric Theatre Hammersmith, the Royal Court Theatre, Tyne Theatre Company and toured internationally with Ballet Rambert. He has designed the sound for over 300 productions including more than 180 for the West Yorkshire Playhouse where he is currently Director of Creative Technology. He received a TMA award in 1992 for Best Designer (Sound) for *Life Is A*

Dream and was nominated for both the Lucille Lortel and the Drama Desk Award for Outstanding Sound Design 2001 for the New York production of *The Unexpected Man*. Recent theatre credits include: *The Postman Always Rings Twice* (Playhouse Theatre); *Ying Tong* (New Ambassadors Theatre); *The Solid Gold Cadillac* (Garrick Theatre); *Brand* (RSC/West End); *Pretending To Be Me* (West Yorkshire Playhouse/West End); *Art* (West End/Broadway/worldwide); *Shockheaded Peter* (Cultural Industry world tour/West End); *The Unexpected Man* (RSC/West End/Broadway/Los Angeles); *Another Country* (Arts Theatre); *Beauty and the Beast, A Midsummer Night's Dream, The Seagull, Victoria, Romeo and Juliet, Twelfth Night, The Roundhouse Season of Late Shakespeare Plays* (RSC); *Three Thousand Troubled Threads* (Stellar Quines/Edinburgh International Festival); *Blues in the Night, A Doll's House, David Copperfield, The 39 Steps, Twelfth Night, My Mother Said I Never Should, Alice in Wonderland, Dead Funny* (West Yorkshire Playhouse); *Homage to Catalonia* (West Yorkshire Playhouse/Northern Stage/Teatre Romea). Video designs for theatre includes: *Der Ring des Nibelungen* (Royal Opera House, Covent Garden); *Three Thousand Troubled Threads* (Stellar Quines/Edinburgh International Festival); *The Solid Gold Cadillac* (West End); *Dracula* (The Touring Consortium); *The Lion, The Witch and the Wardrobe, The Wizard of Oz, Johnson Over Jordan, Crap Dad* (West Yorkshire Playhouse); *Dangerous Corner* (West Yorkshire Playhouse/West End); *Singin' In The Rain* (West Yorkshire Playhouse/

Royal National Theatre/national tour); *The Turk In Italy* (ENO); *The Ring Cycle* (New National Theatre Tokyo); *Il Tabarro, Chorus!* (WNO); *Of Mice and Men* (Mind the Gap). Television includes the sound design for *How wide is your Sky* (Real Life Productions for Channel Four); *Lesley Garrett and Friends At The Movies* (BBC).

Malcolm Rippeth
Lighting Designer

For West Yorkshire Playhouse: *The Lion, the Witch and the Wardrobe, The Bacchae* (with Kneehigh Theatre), *Vodou Nation, Homage to Catalonia* (also Newcastle, Paris and Barcelona), *Medea, Off Camera*. Other theatre credits include: *Hamlet* (ETT/West End); *Romeo and Juliet, John Gabriel Borkman* (ETT); *Nights at the Circus* (Lyric Hammersmith/Kneehigh); *Dick Whittington* (Theatr Clwyd); *Great Expectations, Kaput!, Cinzano and Smirnova's Birthday, The Snow Queen, Noir, Pandora's Box, The Tiger's Bride* (Northern Stage); *Woody Allen's Murder Mysteries* (Croydon Warehouse); *Hay Fever, Macbeth* (York Theatre Royal); *The Lovers, Our Kind of Fun, Lush Life, Toast, Charlie's Trousers, Cooking with Elvis* (Live Theatre, Newcastle); *Foyer, The Selfish Giant* (Leicester Haymarket); *Dealer's Choice* (Salisbury Playhouse); *Coelacanth, Black Cocktail* (Edinburgh Festival); *Bintou* (Arcola); *Abyssinia* (Tiata Fahodzi); *Little Sweet Thing* (Eclipse Theatre); *Antigone at Hell's Mouth* (National Youth Theatre); *Keepers of the Flame* (RSC/Live Theatre). He has also lit *The Ball, La Nuit Intime, La Vie des Fantasmes Érotiques et Esthétiques* (balletLORENT); *Who put*

Bella in the Wych Elm, Infinito Nero
(Almeida Aldeburgh Opera).

George Rodosthenous
Music Consultant

George was awarded a PhD
in Musical Composition at the
University of Leeds (Stanley Burton
Scholarship) and now works there
as a Lecturer in Music Theatre at the
School of Performance and Cultural
Industries. Music for theatre includes:
*The Merchant of Venice, Guy, Bella
and the Beautiful Knight, Orlando,
Iron, Little Eyolf, The Mousetrap,
Professor Wren's Goldfish, Measure
for Measure, Children of a Lesser
God, Gemini, The Visions, The
Gambler, Dumb Wonderland, Closer,
The Propsmaster, The Wedding at the
Eiffel Tower, 21 Years Old at 6 a.m.,
Shelf-life, Love's Sacrifice, A Season
in Hell, Aggression, Schizophrenia,
Sensitivity, In Stillness Movement,
Mosthai*, the original score for the
musical *A Stranger in the House*.
Music for film and television includes:
*The Day Granddad Went Blind, The
10,000th Day, Eve-one morning,
Kirie Proedre, Ta Kopelia*. Credits as
a Musical Director include: *Hysteric
Studs*. Credits as a Director include:
*The Speculator, Howl, Alcestis,
The Sacrifice, Wasted Bodies,
Agamemnon*.

Kay Magson CDG
Casting Director

For the West Yorkshire Playhouse
shows include: *The Magic Paintbrush,
Alice in Wonderland, Twelfth Night,
A Doll's House, Singin' In The Rain*
(and tour), *Martin Guerre* (and
tour), *Bat Boy* (and West End),
*Hamlet, McKellen Ensemble Season,
Blues In The Night, The Madness*
of George III (with Birmingham
Rep), *Popcorn* (original production
with Nottingham Playhouse), *The
Beatification of Area Boy, Enjoy, A
Small Family Business, Johnson Over
Jordan, Eden End, Macbeth, The
Taming of the Shrew, Mister Heracles,
Kes, Electricity, Wind in the Willows,
The Accrington Pals* and many
others. Other theatre credits include:
Assassins (Sheffield Theatres); *The
Solid Gold Cadillac* (Garrick); *Round
The Horne... Revisited* (national
tour); *Dracula* (Bromley/national
tour); *Alfie: The Musical, Queen's
English, The Country Wife, Mother
Goose, Cinderella* (Watford); *Ma
Rainey's Black Bottom, Still Life, The
Astonished Heart, Dr Faustus, The
Odd Couple, Who's Afraid Of Virginia
Woolf?, Chimps And The Tempest*
(Liverpool Everyman Playhouse);
Saved (Bolton Octagon); *Old King
Cole* (Unicorn); *Brassed Off* (Liverpool
Playhouse/Birmingham Rep); *East
Is East* (Pilot/York Theatre Royal/
Octagon Bolton); *Macbeth* (Derby
Playhouse). Kay is a member of the
Casting Directors' Guild.

West Yorkshire Playhouse

Since opening in 1990, the West Yorkshire Playhouse has established a reputation both nationally and internationally as one of Britain's most exciting and active producing theatres, winning awards for everything from its productions to its customer service. The Playhouse provides both a thriving focal point for the communities of West Yorkshire and theatre of the highest standard for audiences throughout the region and beyond. It produces up to 16 of its own shows each year in two auditoria and stages over 1000 performances, workshops, readings and community events, watched by over 250,000 people.

The New Writing programme at the Playhouse develops and produces the best new drama from regional, national and international writers. Since 2001 our programme has been expanded through the collaboration with BBC Northern Exposure. This has created a strong body of writers and new work for theatre, radio and television, and produced such successes as Mark Catley's *Sunbeam Terrace*, the Northern Exposure season of new plays, and *Writing The City*, a co-production with BBC Radio 3. Internationally, the Playhouse co-produces, initiates and leads on a diverse range of projects, including *Huddersfield* by Ugljesa Sajtinac, which has now been seen by audiences in USA, Canada and across Europe, and the *Janus* project which develops and presents 15 new European plays in translation.

Alongside this, high-profile collaborations with companies such as Kneehigh and Improbable Theatre bring highly original new work to the stage. The Playhouse regularly tours productions around Britain and abroad and many have made successful transfers to the West End (including the recent productions of *Ying Tong* and *The Postman Always Rings Twice*).

Together with its work on stage the Playhouse offers extensive and innovative education programmes for children and adults, a wide range of unique community projects and is engaged in the development of culturally diverse arts and artists.

Box Office: 0113 213 7700

www.wyp.org.uk

Maintenance

Frank Monaghan Maintenance Manager

Tony Proudfoot Maintenance Assistant

John Deighton Maintenance Assistant*

Marketing and Sales

Nick Boaden Marketing Manager

Angela Robertson Sales Development Manager

Joanna Down Marketing Officer

Kate Evans Marketing Officer

Neil Armstrong Graphic Design Officer

Caroline Laurent Box Office Manager

Bronia Daniels, Lynn Hudson and **Mel Worman** Duty Supervisors

Rachael Fowler, Rebecca Gibson, Maureen Kershaw, Amy Mackay, Dena Marsh, Sarah McIver, David Salkeld, Holly Thomas and **Sam Ward** Box Office Assistants

Bobby Brook Ambassadors Co-ordinator*

New Writing

Alex Chisholm Literary and Events Manager

Chris Thorpe BBC Writer in Residence

Jodie Marshall Writer on Attachment (05/06)

Oliver Emanuel Writer on Attachment (06)

Paint Shop

Virginia Whiteley Head Scenic Artist

Donna Maria Taylor Freelance Scenic Artist

Performance Staff

Andy Charlesworth and **Jon Murray** Firemen

Andrew Ashdown, Beccy Ashdown, Daisy Babbington, Isobel Bainton, Kathryn Beale, Rachel Blackeby, Alexandra Bradshaw, Andrew Bramma, Jennifer Bramma, Dean Burke, Megan Case, Lindsey Chapman, Megan Christie, Jez Coram, Sarah Cullen, Tony Duggan, Amy Fawdington, Asha France, Averil Frederick, Corinne Furness, Sophie Goodeve, Alison Goodison, Rory Girvan, Andrew Gilpin, Deb Hargrave, Becky Harding, Fiona Heseltine, Rachel Kendall, Jasdeep Lall, Claire Lindus, **Robert Long, Victoria Long, Allan Mawson, Claire McIntyre, Hayley Mort, Jo Murray, Soazig Nicholson, Katie Powers, Sarah Roughley, Monisha Roy, Pam Sandhu, Tim Sharry, Jayne Thompson, Daneill Whyles, Laura Willis** and **Rebekah Wilkes** Attendants*

Press

Rachel Coles Head of Press

Leonie Osborne Acting Head of Press

Robert Farrell Assistant Press Officer

Production Electricians

Matt Young Chief Electrician

David Bennion-Pedley Deputy Chief Electrician

Paul Halgarth, Chris Alexander and **Elizabeth Moran** Electricians

Andrew Bolton Freelance Electrician

Production Management

Suzi Cubbage Production Manager

Eddie de Pledge Production Manager

Dickon Harold Head of Technical Design

Christine Alcock Production Administrator

Props Department

Chris Cully Head of Props

Sarah Barry, Susie Cockram and **Scott Thompson** Prop Makers

Lucy Adams Freelance Prop maker

Restaurant and Bar

Charles Smith Food and Beverage Manager

Michael Montgomery Sous Chef

Louise Poulter Chef de Partie

Kirsty Crerar and **Linda Monaghan** Commis Chefs

Robert Cawood, Lee Moran and **Robert Wright** Kitchen Porters

Diane Kendall and **Pauline Wilkes-Ruan** Restaurant Supervisors

Lee Dennell, Jade Gough, Caron Hawley, Kath Langton* and **Esther Lewis** Restaurant Assistants

Alice Baxter, Rosanna Gordon, Scott Kennedy, Cheryl Lee, Harry Lee, Cati MacKenzie, Rachel Marriner, Julia Mudd, Jessica Rawlins, Sinead Rodgers,

Hayley Smith, Hayley Tong, Justine Tong, William White and Jenny Yan Restaurant Assistants*

Graeme Thompson Bar Supervisor

Terence Whitlam and Graeme Randall Assistant Bar Supervisors*

Elizabeth Carter, Dean Firth, Tracey Hodgetts, Lewis Smith, Giles Green, Dean Firth, Jodie Marshall, Anna Hill, Rory Girvan, Kit Beaumont, Sam Lewis, Andy Ashdown and Karlene Wray Bar Assistants*

Gemma Schoffield Coffee Shop Assistant

Scenic Construction

Andrew Dye Head of Construction

Julian Hibbert and Sally Langford Carpenters and Metal Workers

Jimmy Ragg Carpenter

Andrew Wood Freelance Carpenter

Security

Denis Bray Security Manager

Glenn Slowther Security Officer

Mayfair Security

Sound Department

Andrew Meadows Head of Sound

Martin Pickersgill Deputy Head of Sound

Mathew Angove Assistant Sound Technician

Technical Stage Management

Martin S Ross Technical Stage Manager

Michael Cassidy Deputy Technical Stage Manager

Nidge Solly Stage Technician

David Berrell, Matt Hooban and Matt de Pledge Stage Crew

Theatre Operations

Jeni Chillingsworth House Manager

Pavla Beier, Jonathan Dean, Stuart Simpson* and Sheila Howarth Duty Managers

Wardrobe Department

Stephen Snell Head of Wardrobe

Victoria Marzetti Deputy Head of Wardrobe

Julie Ashworth Head Cutter

Nicole Martin Cutter

Alison Barrett Costume Prop Maker/Dyer

Victoria Harrison, Catherine Lowe and Cathy Royle Wardrobe Assistants

Rowan Martin Costume Hire Manager

Kim Freeland Wig and Make-up Supervisor

Catherine Newton Wardrobe Maintenance / Head Dresser

Stevie Hale-Jones Dresser*

*Denotes part-time

WEST YORKSHIRE PLAYHOUSE
CORPORATE SUPPORTERS

WYPLAY HOUSE

Sponsors of the Arts Development Unit

Media Sponsors

 Scuffer

DIRECTORS CLUB

Executive Members

Associate Members

Director Members

Halifax plc   Incasso Debt Recovery   Provident Financial   Matthew Clark   InBev UK Ltd

West Yorkshire Playhouse gratefully acknowledges support from

CHARITABLE TRUSTS

Audrey and Stanley Burton 1960 Trust
Kenneth Hargreaves Charitable Trust
Clothworkers' Foundation
The Ragdoll Foundation

Harewood Charitable Settlement
The Frances Muers Trust
The Charles Brotherton Trust
Harold Hyam Wingate Foundation

If you would like to learn how your organisation can become involved with the success of the West Yorkshire Playhouse please contact the Development Department on 0113 213 7275.

Introduction to *Scuffer*

After *Sunbeam Terrace* and *Crap Dad* had done pretty well at West Yorkshire Playhouse I was asked for another play; the only criteria given at the time was: 'Make it a comedy, there's not enough comedy being written for the stage.' So I went off to my darkened room and contemplated being funny. I came up with an idea, a very elaborate, surreal and theatrical idea. I spent the next few weeks carefully plotting it out, giving it structure and depth, pouring my all into it. The end product was very unlike my previous two plays; I felt that, as a writer, I was evolving. Then came the point of submission and I recalled another piece of the initial conversation: 'Give us a couple of ideas to go on.' So I spent the next ten minutes coming up with the first thing I could think of. That ten minutes of panic was entitled *Scuffer*. The lesson I learnt from this? If it ain't broke don't fix it.

'Scuffer' is a term I have used for many years and which has been used against me for just as long. It relates to someone who is any or all of the following: scruffy, poor, lazy, dirty, prone to petty theft. I know I heard it long before the inclusion of the word chav in the English language and want to clearly state that my scuffer is not a chav. He is not making a statement with his attire, he is simply trying to blend into his surroundings with the minimal income he has.

Scuffer is all about discovering what's beneath the surface of a kid who is ridiculed and dismissed, not just by those who know him, but by society in general (especially the media). It's no great political statement, I just wanted to show the beauty and tragedy that makes up someone like this. I drew on my experiences of working with lads in the care system and schools of Leeds.

I worked with Mic Pool on *Crap Dad*. He designed projections to cover the set and create the backdrops – much to my chagrin this innovative design got more coverage than the play but nevertheless I was keen to further this style of working and asked Mic how far he could take it. 'Very' was the reply. Knowing that there isn't going to be thirty seconds of darkness between each scene is quite liberating for a playwright, it meant I could do movie-like cutaways and, more importantly, set the scenes wherever the hell I wanted. For anybody wanting to stage this play without such technical support I apologise in advance.

Ultimately, *Scuffer* is a comedy, albeit a dark one. It has a very simple narrative (get money or have legs broken) colourful characters and a great set. As long as people enjoy it and feel they have spent their money wisely, I'll be happy. But if you take away a deeper understanding of the plight of the young and poor in this nation, if you perchance befriend someone like Scuffer...don't have a go at me if you get robbed!

Mark Catley

SCUFFER

First published in 2006 by Oberon Books Ltd
521 Caledonian Road, London N7 9RH
Tel: 020 7607 3637 / Fax: 020 7607 3629
e-mail: info@oberonbooks.com
www.oberonbooks.com

A catalogue record for this book is available from the British
Library.

ISBN: 1 84002 664 2

Printed in Great Britain by Antony Rowe Ltd, Chippenham.

Characters

DANNY

The Scuffer, early twenties, clearly malnourished in his younger years. Seemingly oblivious to the complexities of the world, naïve, slightly dopey but has an intelligence he is desperate to quell for fear of realisation. Not thinking is easier than facing his past and present. A deeply loving man.

AMY

Danny's ex. Younger than him (17-ish) but much more worldly. Has incredible support from her family but that hasn't stopped her making some big mistakes. Feisty, ambitious but under the mistaken impression that her salvation from the estate lies with somebody with a penis rather than herself. Very astute and brave.

JACK

Amy's dad. Formally a scary hard man, not afraid of a scrap but, due to maturity and illness, has mended his ways to become all heart. Can still struggle with displaying emotion but has a huge capacity to love…probably making up for the lost years. Confident, empathetic and brave. Loves his daughter unequivocally.

CATHY

(late twenties / early thirties) Debt collector and proud(ish) member of the White family, villains with notoriety. Afraid of nothing, she seems to have taken on her role with relish, but, behind closed doors is a desperately lonely young woman.

CAULDRON

(mid- to late twenties) Sick bastard. A villain with the full backing of the White family. Drug, porn and prostitution are his racket and he loves his job. Deep down he hates himself but he never goes that far down. Realises that Amy was his one chance for redemption.

Others:
ARTIST, MAN IN SUIT, OLD LADY IN CHEMIST, SMACKHEAD, DEALER

Setting

Could be any city with a change of dialect but for my purposes it is Leeds with the suburb of Beeston being where they all live.

The original production used projections to denote the various settings.

Music

It was always envisioned that Danny would be into the music of Stevie Wonder but copyright prevented this for the original production. Alternatives are: Neil Diamond, Roy Orbison, Willie Nelson, Marvin Gaye, Lionel Ritchie, Al Green or Elvis.

Chapter One
THE I IN TEAM

SCENE 1 – DANNY AND AMY'S FLAT

DANNY has just got up, he is wearing just boxer shorts (grey). The flat is a mess.

DANNY: Amy?

> *He looks around.*

> Amy?

> *He looks for her things, they are gone.*

> (*More distressed.*) Amy?

> *There is a knock at the door. DANNY, relieved, looks for his keys, he can't find them.*

> Hang on babe, can't find me keys.

> *He continues looking.*

> Haven't you got yours?

> *No answer. DANNY gets suspicious, he goes to the door.*

> Amy?

CATHY: (*Pause.*) Yeah.

DANNY: (*Panicking.*) No you're not.

> *CATHY bangs on door, tries to break in, but can't, she starts to count down from ten.*

> *DANNY panics, he rushes around looking for somewhere to hide. He goes to the window, looks out.*

> (*Mutters.*) Fucking tower blocks!

> *DANNY hides.*

CATHY: Right!

> *A power drill can be heard, drilling out DANNY's lock. DANNY comes out of his hiding place and tries to find a weapon (like*

*Pulp Fiction, but fork, spatula, large book and then frying pan),
and hides again. CATHY kicks open the door. She stands in the
doorway, power drill in one hand, cig hanging out of her mouth.
She puts the drill down and politely closes the door.*

Ashtray.

DANNY sheepishly stands, frying pan in hand.

(*Takes her time.*) I've had breakfast.

*DANNY takes the frying pan to CATHY; she uses it as an
ashtray. She stubs out the cig whilst DANNY holds it in his hand.
When she has finished he puts the frying pan down.*

Shall we begin?

DANNY: Yeah, if you want.

*CATHY launches herself at him, DANNY is kneeling in front
of CATHY. She has his little finger bent back. She viciously
bends his finger back, we hear the snap. DANNY screams, looks
incredulous, then faints. CATHY looks disappointed.*

CATHY: It's always the men that faint.

She sits, takes a bottle of water out of her pocket and drinks.

SCENE 2 – AMY'S PARENTS' BATHROOM

AMY is sat looking at her mobile phone.

AMY: Ten, nine, eight, seven, six, five, four, three, two, one.
(*She looks at a pregnancy test.*) Aw tits!

SCENE 3 – DANNY AND AMY'S FLAT

*CATHY, sat on bed. She takes a drink then squirts some on DANNY's
head. He doesn't move, she laughs. She repeats the move, taking aim like
a cowboy, still DANNY doesn't move.*

CATHY: (*Bored now.*) Come on prick, what's it take?

*The post arrives, one letter falls to the floor. CATHY doesn't move
whilst this happens and is wary. Suddenly DANNY sits up.*

DANNY: (*Cheerful.*) Giro!

DANNY stands and walks over. Goes to pick up his mail when he notices his little finger sticking out at a strange angle.

Aargh!

He notices CATHY.

Oh?

CATHY: I'll give you a minute.

DANNY stands, gormless, suddenly it dawns on him. He goes to open the door with his bad hand.

DANNY: Aargh! You bastard.

He opens door with his other hand and runs out, CATHY follows him.

A few moments later, she leads him back into the room by his ear.

CATHY: Come, take a seat.

She sits him down.

DANNY: I were just going to the cashpoint Cathy!

CATHY: Aye.

DANNY: I was! I swear to you...

CATHY: Shush.

DANNY stops talking.

Now, keep it shut whilst I do the formalities.

DANNY nods. CATHY pulls out a contract from her pocket.

(*Waving contract.*) Exactly six months ago, you borrowed two hundred and fifty quid, is that right?

DANNY: Yeah.

CATHY: What was our repayment agreement?

DANNY: Forty quid a month, for a year.

CATHY: How much have you paid so far?

DANNY: (*Sheepish.*) Sixty-five.

CATHY: And how much should you have paid so far?

DANNY: Two hundred and forty.

CATHY: Correct rain man. (*Beat.*) You've broken our loan agreement, yeah?

DANNY: Yeah.

CATHY: And what was the loan secured against?

DANNY looks up, scared.

What was the loan secured against Danny?

DANNY: (*Nervous laugh.*) My legs, but…

CATHY: Yes, your legs, quite right.

DANNY: You're not gonna break my legs? (*Pause.*) Are you gonna break my legs?

CATHY: Unless payment is received, in full…yes. That's eight hundred quid.

DANNY: But I only borrowed…

CATHY: Quiet! You little retard. Interest, late payment penalties and wasting my time for six fucking months has incurred various hidden charges. So, no arguments. If you've not got it, I break them knots in thread you call legs. You with me?

DANNY: Yeah.

CATHY: Today.

DANNY: You're having a laugh!

CATHY: I don't know how to.

DANNY: (*Pause.*) All right…today.

CATHY stares at DANNY.

What?

CATHY: The thought has just occurred to you, hasn't it?

DANNY: What thought?

CATHY: To do a runner.

DANNY: No, no not at all.

CATHY: Oh it has! Sure as shit it has. Let me read something to you.

CATHY looks at the contract.

Miss Amy Douglas of 22 Westbury Road is hereby named… (*Looks at DANNY.*) Do you know where I'm going with this?

DANNY nods.

Good. (*Beat.*) So everything's clear?

DANNY nods.

DANNY: (*Sad.*) Yeah, crystal. What time do you want it?

CATHY: (*Raises her eyebrows.*) Ever the optimist. (*Beat.*) Tonight will do, late on.

DANNY: There's no need to bring Amy into it, I don't want her to know.

CATHY: You settle up and there'll be no need.

DANNY: Aye.

CATHY: So…mongy, let's see if we can't lighten the load for you.

DANNY looks quizzical.

You got owt you wanna sell to me?

DANNY's eyes brighten.

DANNY: Oh aye, yeah.

He looks around. Goes to TV.

TV and video combi.

CATHY: No DVD?

DANNY: No.

CATHY: Scruff. (*Looks at TV.*) Thirty.

DANNY: Thirty?!

CATHY: This isn't Bargain Hunt bitch! There's no bartering.

DANNY: Right.

CATHY: Owt else?

DANNY thinks, CATHY unplugs the TV and picks it up.

DANNY: I've got loads of books.

CATHY: What the fuck have you got books for?

DANNY: I just have.

CATHY: Nah, can't do owt wi' books. (*Beat.*) Jewellery I can.

DANNY: Haven't got none.

CATHY eyes his necklace.

CATHY: What's that then?

DANNY: Not this.

CATHY: Off!

DANNY, resigned, fiddles with the chain.

DANNY: It's stuck.

CATHY: Bollox.

CATHY undoes it with ease.

(*Disdain.*) Stuck?

DANNY: Me dad bought me it.

CATHY holds the chain, weighs it in her hand.

CATHY: What the fuck is it?

DANNY: Gold.

CATHY: Is it bollox! It weighs nowt. It's diet gold! Gold-ish, I can't believe it's not gold.

DANNY: It were me dad's.

CATHY puts it in her pocket.

CATHY: Now I'm your daddy. Twenty. (*Beat.*) Computer?

DANNY shakes his head.

Hi fi?

DANNY: Cash Converters.

CATHY: Gypo. (*Beat.*) CDs?

DANNY: No.

CATHY goes to pick up half a dozen CDs.

CATHY: What's these then? (*Looks through CDs.*) Stevie Wonder?

DANNY: I like him.

CATHY: Where's the scruffy bastard classics? Gatecrasher? Happy Hardcore? Misery of Sound?

DANNY: I like Stevie Wonder.

CATHY: (*Pockets them.*) Fiver.

SCENE 4 – AMY'S PARENTS' HOUSE – DINING ROOM

AMY's parents house. Dad, JACK, is sat, eating a sandwich. AMY waits on the outskirts.

AMY: (*To herself.*) There's no point in pissing around is there? (*To JACK.*) Dad?

JACK: (*Mouth full.*) What?

AMY sits opposite him.

AMY: How are you?

JACK stares at her.

JACK: Cut the shit, what's up?

AMY: (*Cute.*) Do you love me?

JACK: Every now and then.

AMY: Even when I mess up?

JACK: No.

AMY: Aww, you're ace you.

JACK: Amy, love, you're just too ugly to eat in front of.

AMY: Stop it! You'll make me blush.

JACK: How big have you messed up?

AMY: Pretty damn big.

JACK zones out and stares into space. AMY notices and waves her hand in front of his face.

Dad?

She waves her hand in front of his face. Nothing. She waits, deliberating.

(*To herself.*) It's just rude not to.

She takes the sandwich out of his hand and puts it on his head. Then she covers her head with her jumper. Moments pass and JACK returns to consciousness. He jumps at AMY's appearance, the sandwich goes everywhere. AMY is laughing.

JACK: (*Angry.*) Stop doing that!!

AMY: Doing what?

Still laughing, she pulls her jumper back down.

JACK: You're gonna clean that up and make me another butty.

AMY: Yeah, course I will.

JACK: You're not supposed to mock the afflicted.

AMY: It's fun though.

JACK: Why are you bugging me?

AMY: Oh yeah, I'm pregnant.

JACK falters, slightly.

JACK: Right. (*Beat.*) Is it Danny's?

AMY: Course it is!

JACK shakes his head slowly, AMY nods her reply.

JACK: You sure?

AMY: Positive.

JACK: Why?

AMY: Danny's not father material... I'm not gonna be a single mum.

JACK: If you're sure.

She nods again. JACK stands, gets his wallet, shouts through to kitchen.

Denise! We're not off to the caravan this weekend love. (*Pause, listening.*) Tough!

He goes back to AMY. Hands her two hundred quid. Sits. They look at one another.

Get yourself to the clinic then.

AMY: I will.

JACK: Good. Now go get me another sandwich and tell your mam we need some more radishes.

AMY: I love you dad.

JACK: Aye, well, I'm lovable aren't I?

AMY kisses her dad's cheek and exits. JACK picks sandwich off the floor and dusts it off.

SCENE 5 – DANNY AND AMY'S FLAT

CATHY is laden with goods, including some clothes. She is at the door.

CATHY: Right then, dickhead. I'll see thee tonight, kicking out time. Make sure you're here.

DANNY: (*Stood dejectedly.*) I will be.

CATHY: And no welcoming committee Danny, you really don't want to go there.

DANNY nods.

I'll be keeping an eye on you today.

CATHY exits. DANNY turns away from the door, he is angry and upset.

DANNY: You fat bitch! Transvestite looking he/she…

CATHY enters through the door.

CATHY: Ere!

DANNY jumps.

I nearly forgot your giro.

CATHY picks the giro off the floor.

Six-twenty left. (*Beat.*) By the way, I've been called worse.

CATHY leaves.

DANNY: Bollox.

DANNY puts his head in his hands. He's panicking.

Shit, shit, shit!

He shakes off the malaise. He gets himself ready to leave. Tracky bottoms, Reebok classic trainers, Rockport jumper, baseball cap.

Six-twenty…six hundred and twenty squid. (*Pause.*) Fuck! Come on dickhead.

He is dressed.

It's time to do what I do best. (*Beat.*) Let someone else sort it out. (*Nods.*) Let's go to work.

Reservoir Dogs music plays, DANNY goes to leave the flat. He stops, music stops. He tucks his tracksuit bottoms into his socks.

Sweet. (*Exits.*)

SCENE 6 – AMY'S PARENTS' HOUSE

JACK is sat, still eating sandwich. DANNY comes to the door, looking dishevelled.

DANNY knocks at the door. JACK answers it.

DANNY: Alright Jack? Is Amy in?

JACK stares at DANNY, without answering. DANNY thinks he has zoned out and waves his hand in front of JACK's face. JACK grabs his hand, DANNY is shocked.

Aargh, ow. That's my bad hand Jack.

JACK moves DANNY's hand closer, he examines it.

JACK: What happened?

DANNY: I broke it. (*Beat.*) I thought you'd zoned out Jack, sorry.

JACK lets his hand go.

Is Amy in?

JACK moves away from the door and lets DANNY enter, AMY walks in the room, with her coat on, she stops and stares at DANNY.

Hiya.

AMY and DANNY stare at one another. JACK remains at the open door.

Amy?

AMY: Danny?

DANNY: You weren't there this morning.

AMY: No.

DANNY: You've taken your stuff.

AMY: I know. I've moved back in here.

DANNY: Why?

AMY: (*Disgusted.*) Eeergh! What the hell is that?

DANNY: What?

AMY: Your finger, why's it sticking out like that?

DANNY: It's broken.

AMY: How?

DANNY: (*Looks uncomfortably at JACK.*) I'm in a bit of bother… wi some money lenders.

AMY: Someone did that to you?

DANNY: Yeah. Why've you left me?

AMY: I don't want to talk about it Danny. Why'd they break your finger?

DANNY: Cos I owe em eight hundred quid. Gotta pay it by tonight or they're gonna break me legs.

AMY: Who is?

DANNY: I told you! Money lenders. Why don't you want to talk about us?

AMY is perplexed.

AMY: Danny, shut up! Your telling me that someone's gonna break your legs tonight if you don't get em eight hundred quid?

DANNY: Well it's six twenty now, I sold some stuff…you're lucky you took your things…

AMY gives him a look.

Yes, my legs will be broke.

AMY: And doesn't this bother you?

DANNY: Course it does, but it also bothers me that me bird's dumped me for no good reason, we didn't even have an argument.

AMY: What you gonna do?

DANNY: (*Louder.*) Try and talk to her!

AMY: (*Louder.*) Forget about me!

DANNY: (*Childish.*) I don't wanna.

AMY notices JACK stood at the door.

AMY: Do you want some popcorn?

JACK: No, I'm alright. (*Pause. Impasse.*) I'm off out.

JACK exits.

AMY: Listen Danny, me and you can talk later, I'm not going anywhere, what you gonna do?

DANNY: Dunno do I? Can't get another loan can I? There's only them'd borrow me it.

AMY: Are they really gonna break your legs or are they just trying to shit you up?

DANNY: Oh no, she meant it.

AMY: She?

DANNY: Yeah. Cathy White. Terry's sister.

AMY: White?

DANNY: Yeah.

AMY: Fuck.

DANNY: My thought exactly, they're gonna cripple me Amy.

AMY: I don't know what to suggest.

DANNY: I did have one idea.

AMY: What?

DANNY: Maybe go ask Cauldron.

AMY: Cauldron? You're having a laugh?

DANNY: I've got nowt to lose, what's the worst he'll say? No?

AMY: He hates you Danny.

DANNY: Yeah. (*Sheepish.*) That's why I were hoping you'd come with me.

AMY: Me?

DANNY: Yeah, you used to go out with him, he don't hate you.

AMY: But I hate him. You forgotten what he did?

DANNY: No.

AMY: And you'd still go asking him for a favour?

DANNY: (*Beat.*) No, I weren't thinking straight.

AMY: Damn right. It's a bad idea all round, don't go asking him for owt.

DANNY: I don't know what else to do.

AMY: (*Cruel.*) Do a runner Danny. (*Busies herself.*)

DANNY: Aw that's nice is that. It's not enough that you move out for no reason, you want me to leave town.

AMY: I don't want you to get your legs broken, that's all.

DANNY: Well I'm staying, cos I wouldn't do that to you.

AMY: Do what?

DANNY: (*Caught out.*) Nowt, forget it.

AMY: What you on about? You wouldn't do what to me?

DANNY: Look Amy, are we gonna talk about us or what?

AMY: No, not now Danny, I've got things to do and so have you obviously.

DANNY: (*Dejected.*) Right, well I'll be off then. (*Turns to leave.*) Cheers.

AMY: Ere.

DANNY stops and turns, hopeful.

When did you borrow this money?

DANNY: (*Thrown out.*) I can't remember.

AMY: Were we together?

DANNY: I've got to go.

AMY: Danny Wild, I am talking to you. Did you borrow this money when we were together?

DANNY: (*Sheepish.*) I might have done.

AMY: I don't remember you having any money…ever! What did you spend it on?

DANNY: Erm…

DANNY is panicking, he looks at AMY.

Bye.

DANNY quickly exits.

AMY: Danny! I'll find out you know.

He has gone.

Wanker!

SCENE 7 – CATHY'S HOUSE

Enter CATHY, with bag of DANNY's belongings. She places a wad of notes in a jar. She sits, looks around, checks her mobile. Bored. She gets out DANNY's CDs.

Bookies: JACK is in bookies, writing out a betting slip.

SCENE 8 – PUB

CAULDRON is on the fruit machine, DANNY is stood near him.

CAULDRON: Tha's got some big balls asking that of me.

DANNY: I know mate, I know, but I'm not taking liberties, I'm in a bad situation here.

CAULDRON: Aye.

Long pause.

DANNY: So?

CAULDRON finishes his game and returns to his seat, DANNY joins him. CAULDRON is drinking lager and a neat spirit chaser.

CAULDRON: What you gonna do for me?

DANNY: Whatever. If you need anything doing. (*Pause.*) I'll do deliveries.

CAULDRON: I've got joeys who'll do that for skag.

DANNY: Well, I'll do owt.

CAULDRON: Would you suck me cock?

DANNY: (*Thrown out.*) What?

CAULDRON bursts out laughing. DANNY is relieved.

CAULDRON: Behave man. (*Serious again.*) Would you kill someone?

DANNY: Are you still joking?

CAULDRON: (*Wasn't joking.*) Yeah of course. Just trying to work out how much you want it.

DANNY: Well I'm asking me bird's ex, that should tell you something.

CAULDRON: It does. (*Beat.*) I just don't know what you can do for it.

DANNY: I'll pay you back.

CAULDRON: It's stupid statements like that got you into this mess. Why would I be any different?

DANNY: Because it's you Cauldron mate, I wouldn't mess you about. It'll get paid back.

CAULDRON: Ere, what's your knob like? I'm always looking for actors.

DANNY: What?

CAULDRON: (*Holds out his thumb and little finger stretched out as far as possible.*) Do this.

DANNY tries it with his bad hand first, then the other. CAULDRON scrutinizes and measures his own against it.

Nah.

DANNY: Cheers.

CAULDRON: How much you need then?

DANNY: Six twenty.

CAULDRON: (*Slowly smiles, takes his time.*) Seems fair enough.

DANNY: For real?

CAULDRON: Yeah man. (*Goes into back pocket.*) Just cos of some split arse, don't mean two blokes can't do business. I've known you years Danny.

DANNY: Yeah man, we're old friends! Cheers for this Cauldron, big time.

CAULDRON removes a huge bundle of notes and slowly counts out £620.

CAULDRON: How is little Amy anyhow?

DANNY: Oh, she's alright. (*Beat.*) She's in a bit of a pod wi me, truth be known.

CAULDRON: Why's that?

DANNY: Dunno, she won't tell me.

CAULDRON: Did you give her a crack?

DANNY: No.

CAULDRON: She's a mouthy one her. I had to chin her myself once or twice.

DANNY: (*Uncomfortable.*) Yeah.

DANNY is eyeing the money, CAULDRON takes his time.

CAULDRON: Do you know what amazes me about young lasses these days?

DANNY: What's that?

CAULDRON: Little princesses one and all. They want you to buy em nice things take em out for meals…look after em like.

DANNY nods.

I mean that's their choice, to do that. That's why they go out with older blokes, but, you try and get owt off them. Get em to make you some snap, iron a pair of kegs, come on their face, it's all 'What do you think I am?' Well, I'll tell you what they are, they're kept women, pure and simple and I want some pay back for spending me hard earned, you know?

DANNY: Aye.

CAULDRON: Double standards. You wanna be an independent bitch who don't do fuck all for a bloke then don't have me walking round town buying half of Miss Selfridges. You wanna be independent, then be independent. Spend your own bastard money. (*Pause.*) Empowerment, they call it. Young women are empowered, my fucking ring piece they are! They're lazy bitches who want it all wi fuck all effort. (*Beat.*) Amy'll sort herself out man, they can't cope on their own. (*Beat.*) Right. I've lost count now.

CAULDRON starts counting the money out again.

I'll tell you summat though, they know what they're doing in the sack, eh?

DANNY: Oh aye.

CAULDRON: Fucking hell fire. I had this little un, last week, born for porn. Proper tidy little titties, Brazilian downstairs. Fucking Mardi Gras big lad, I tell you!

DANNY: Nice one.

CAULDRON: (*Pause.*) Does Amy still like her back door kicking in?

DANNY: What?

CAULDRON: She'd need a few drinks down her first. I liked to pop a couple of vodkas in her breezer, always guaranteed a bit of back door action that.

CAULDRON stops and looks at DANNY, who doesn't know how to react.

You alright?

DANNY: Yeah.

CAULDRON: (*Indicates money.*) You still want this?

DANNY: Course.

CAULDRON: Nearly there.

CAULDRON counts in silence.

Six twenty.

CAULDRON pushes the money into the middle of the table and puts the rest back in his pocket.

DANNY: You're a star Cauldron.

DANNY reaches for the money. CAULDRON grabs his bad hand.

CAULDRON: One thing I hate more than prissy little split arse. (*Beat.*) That's wankers like you.

DANNY: (*In pain but trying not to show it.*) I don't know what you mean. That's me bad hand mate...

CAULDRON: Don't mate me you fucking crank. Steal a bird away from me then come asking for a favour? Take, take, take, that's all it is wi you scruffy bastards.

DANNY: I didn't know she was with anyone Cauldron, she never said.

CAULDRON: I don't give a shit about her. It's the principle. You had one over on me and, much to my stupidity, I let you get away wi it. Then what do you do? You come tapping money off me. Piss-taker you are.

DANNY: I'm not, I just thought you might be…

CAULDRON: You thought wrong.

DANNY: But you said you would.

CAULDRON: I say a lot of things I don't mean. Now, before I send you packing to have your legs snapped.

Still holding DANNY's hand, CAULDRON tips his drink over the money. He picks up a lighter and burns the money.

I'd rather watch it burn than lend it to a scuffer like you.

DANNY: You fucking idiot!

DANNY tries to struggle free but CAULDRON twists his arm. DANNY is in serious pain.

Get off me!

Enter AMY, she calmly walks over to the chaotic scene and pours the lager over the burning money. CAULDRON pushes the whimpering DANNY away and faces AMY.

CAULDRON: I was just talking about you baby.

AMY: Come on Danny, let's get out of here.

CAULDRON: Who do think you are little madam?

AMY: Piss off Cauldron.

CAULDRON: Oi! Play nice.

AMY: Do I have to remind you how old I was when we got together? Eh? I might shout it out by accident…nonce. (*To DANNY.*) Get up Danny, we're leaving.

CAULDRON is silent. DANNY gets to his feet and walks towards AMY, silently they leave. CAULDRON sits.

CAULDRON: (*Shaking his head.*) Not twice. (*Looks at the ashes of his money.*) I'm fucking thick sometimes me.

SCENE 9 – CATHY'S HOUSE

CATHY is dancing to 'Superstition' by Stevie Wonder.

Bookies: JACK is watching a horse race finish, he shows some happiness when his horse wins.

SCENE 10 – THE CHEMIST'S

An OLD LADY is working behind counter, DANNY and AMY enter.

DANNY: Thank you.

AMY is looking out for CAULDRON following them.

I said thank you.

AMY: I heard.

The coast is clear. AMY turns on DANNY.

What did I tell you eh?

DANNY: Don't go to Cauldron.

AMY: So what do you do?

DANNY: I'm desperate Amy!

AMY: Suicidal?

DANNY: Nearly.

AMY grabs his hand, DANNY yelps.

AMY: Go to casualty.

DANNY: Not a chance.

AMY: Get a bandage on it then.

DANNY is staring at AMY.

What?

DANNY: How come you saved me?

AMY: What did you spend the money on?

DANNY: (*Pause.*) Touché.

AMY: Come on then.

They begin looking around the chemists.

DANNY: (*Whispering.*) Amy.

AMY comes over.

AMY: What?

DANNY: I haven't got any money to pay for this.

AMY: No surprise there. I'll pay it.

DANNY: You sure?

AMY: Yeah.

DANNY: We could just rob it.

AMY: No.

DANNY: Well, look. It's just some old biddy on the till, the rest of em are doing needle exchange round the side.

AMY: I said I'll get it.

DANNY: Ok.

AMY: (*Going back to the aisle.*) Bandages.

DANNY: Painkillers.

AMY: I've got em.

DANNY: Condoms?

AMY: Fuck off Danny.

DANNY looks around again. AMY goes to counter and starts paying. DANNY opens a packet of tights and puts one over his head. He ducks out of sight.

OLD LADY: Oh, hello again.

AMY: Hiya love.

OLD LADY: Seven forty-eight please luvvy.

AMY hands her a tenner. OLD LADY counts out the change.

And two is ten.

AMY: Thank you.

OLD LADY: You're welcome flower.

AMY turns and walks away from counter, she looks around for DANNY. DANNY stands and walks purposefully towards the counter. AMY spots him and tackles him to the ground. She sits on top of him, facing each other.

AMY: What the hell are you doing?

DANNY: It's me only chance babe, I grab the cash, problem solved.

AMY: No Danny, this isn't you.

DANNY: I'm desperate!

AMY: But what if you get caught?

DANNY: So I get arrested? She can't break me legs if I'm in nick.

AMY: Stop being a div!

DANNY: What do you care? You've sacked me!

AMY: (*Furious.*) This is why I don't want to be with you!

OLD LADY looks over the counter at DANNY and AMY on the floor.

OLD LADY: Everything all right love?

AMY: It's fine…we're just talking.

OLD LADY: (*Pleasant.*) Right you are.

DANNY: What you mean?

AMY: You're gonna make me spell it out aren't you?

DANNY: Yeah, do it slowly, cos I'm a bit thick!

AMY: It's you! I don't know what goes on in your head Danny but I don't wanna live like this no more. I don't wanna spend my days worrying about what crazy shit you're gonna get us into. It's not exciting any more, I used to think we lived on the edge. We don't, we're way past the edge, we're in a… (*Struggles for the right word.*) black thingy… empty and that.

DANNY: Void.

AMY: What?

DANNY: We're in a void, that's what you're trying to say.

AMY: Yeah. And this…you're intelligent really, you're bright…

DANNY: Don't start that shit!

AMY: You are though! Why are you living like this? Why you making me live like this?

DANNY: I'm doing my best!

AMY: Robbing a chemist is your best?

DANNY: Extenuating circumstances!

AMY: It's not like I want a riverside apartment or a frigging Range Rover, we live in a high rise with smackheads, ex mental patients and that old biddy who drinks her own piss. (*Beat.*) I'd just like to think I deserve somewhere in-between.

At this point a SMACKHEAD enters with a mask on. DANNY and AMY stop and look up. He loiters near the counter.

SMACKHEAD reaches over the counter and is trying to get in the till.

OLD LADY: 'Ere, what you doing?

DANNY and AMY witness the scene.

OLD LADY traps the SMACKHEAD's hand in the till, he screams in pain. OLD LADY grabs SMACKHEAD's hair and bangs his head on the counter. He stumbles back, OLD LADY walks out from behind the counter and kicks him in the balls.

You cheeky little bastard! Get out! Go on.

She kicks his arse out of the shop, she turns to AMY and DANNY.

Sorry about that. Very embarrassing.

AMY and DANNY look at one another. AMY removes DANNY's tights.

Gets worse don't it?

AMY: It does love.

OLD LADY: See, I'll bet he's not a bad lad really, just got in with the wrong crowd or something.

AMY: Yeah, probably.

OLD LADY: Such a shame.

AMY: It is. See you later love.

OLD LADY: Aye take care.

AMY and DANNY leave.

SCENE 11 – CATHY'S HOUSE

CATHY is sat, bored again. Alarm on her mobile goes, she switches it off and gets her coat. She leaves the house.

SCENE 12 – OUTSIDE CHEMIST, STREET CORNER, BUS SHELTER

AMY and DANNY are sat on a bench. AMY is bandaging DANNY's hand.

AMY: You glad you didn't do it?

DANNY: Yeah, course.

AMY: Cos, you're a lot of things Danny, but you're not a robber.

DANNY: Yeah.

AMY: (*Indicating hand.*) Looks painful.

DANNY: Hurts like a bastard.

AMY grabs it and pulls it. DANNY screeches.

Aargh! What you doing?

AMY: Resetting it.

DANNY: Why are women out to hurt me today?

AMY: I'm gonna bandage it now, should make it better.

DANNY: (*AMY starts bandaging, DANNY stares at her.*) It makes it better you being here.

AMY: (*Soft.*) Don't.

Long silence.

DANNY: I'm sorry.

AMY: For what?

DANNY: Being me.

AMY: Don't be silly, what you saying that for?

DANNY: I always knew I was on borrowed time with you. (*AMY looks quizzically at him.*) You're way out of my league. From day one I've known, so I thought to myself, May as well enjoy it while it lasts. Make the most of it.

AMY: Stop it! You know the rejects I've been out with before you...

DANNY: Yeah, and you were above their league 'n all, that's why you're not with em. I'm just another waster to add to your list.

AMY: You're not like them Danny, you're miles nicer than likes of Cauldron.

DANNY: But you're still sacking me.

AMY: It's more complicated than that.

DANNY: It's black and white Amy. You don't wanna be with me, therefore I'm not good enough for you, it's all right, I understand.

AMY: No it's grey Danny, everything's fucking grey. (*Finished bandaging.*) How's that feel?

DANNY: (*Melodramatic.*) Like a dagger through my heart.

AMY: Your hand.

DANNY: I know. (*Looks at his hand.*) Feels better.

AMY suddenly feels sick.

You look pale.

AMY: Need the loo.

DANNY: You all right?

AMY: Yeah. I'm gonna have to use them public bogs.

DANNY: You're kidding.

AMY: I don't have much choice. (*Goes to leave.*)

DANNY: Be careful. (*Beat, panic.*) Amy!

AMY: What?!

DANNY: You coming back?

AMY: (*Sigh.*) Yes.

> *AMY exits. DANNY examines the job AMY's done on his hand.*
> *CATHY sits next to him.*

CATHY: That looks nasty. Wanking accident?

DANNY: Aw fuck. (*Beat.*) I'm not gonna do a runner Cathy.

CATHY: How's the treasure hunt going?

DANNY: I'll get it.

CATHY: I told you, I don't mind either way. (*Beat.*) Ere!
That Stevie Wonder's better than I thought... I only knew
'Ebony and Ivory' and, what were other shit one?

DANNY: 'I just called to say I love you.'

CATHY: That's the badger. They were the only ones I knew of
his... Proper shite!

DANNY: They're not his best.

CATHY: But there's some right funky tunes on there.

DANNY: Yeah.

CATHY: (*Squeezes his knee.*) You sure you're not waiting for a
bus to get out of here?

DANNY: I'm sure.

CATHY: Cos I were just passing and saw you, and I thought,
'That fucker looks like he might be doing a nash.'

DANNY: I'm not.

CATHY: Cos there's a certain Miss Douglas who'll be getting a
visit if you do.

DANNY: There's no need.

CATHY: Well that's great, cos I take no pleasure in hurting little girls. Have I just seen her?

DANNY: No.

CATHY: Her name's familiar. She your bird then?

DANNY: You'll never have to meet her Cathy, cos I'll be there tonight, with or without.

JACK enters and sits on the other side of DANNY. DANNY notices and is shocked.

CATHY: Where you going then?

DANNY: I was just sitting here.

JACK holds his hand out to CATHY.

JACK: Jack.

CATHY: (*Ignoring the hand.*) Do I know you?

JACK: I think it's hard enough for the lad without you breathing down his neck all day.

CATHY: Who's this?

DANNY: It's Jack.

CATHY thinks. JACK is nonchalant. DANNY is shitting himself. Long silence.

CATHY: (*Quiet.*) Thought I warned you about back-up?

DANNY: You did.

CATHY: So...why is this big prick fucking with me?

JACK: I'm not...

CATHY: (*Stands, suddenly very loud.*) Shut the fuck up!

JACK is almost amused, he raises his hands in supplication.

(*To DANNY.*) I swear to God Danny, you try owt on tonight I'll have you shot in the face, you with me?

DANNY: Yeah.

CATHY: (*To JACK.*) And I don't wanna see you there, else you'll be getting the same.

JACK: Message understood.

Long silence as JACK and DANNY watch her leave. Despite her aggression, CATHY has been scared off.

JACK: If me mam were still alive, she'd have had her.

DANNY: Er…

JACK hands DANNY a small wad of money.

JACK: Don't let Denise know I've been gambling.

DANNY: What's this Jack?

JACK: Eighty quid.

DANNY: Really?

JACK: So, it's not as much as you need but it'll help.

DANNY: Cheers Jack! That's well nice of you.

JACK: Aye, maybe it could've been more but I only got the one decent tip…

DANNY: No, this is ace, but I don't think…

JACK: I'm not gonna start anything with Cathy, that would just make it worse for you.

DANNY: (*Smiles his thanks.*) Are you sure you want me to have this?

JACK: Yeah.

DANNY: Why?

JACK just smiles and shrugs at a confused DANNY.

AMY re-enters.

AMY: Dad?

JACK: Super Dad if you don't mind.

AMY notices the money in DANNY's hands.

AMY: Where'd you get that?

DANNY: Erm… I bumped into an old mate of mine, he lent me it.

JACK: That's very noble of you lad. (*To AMY.*) I got a decent tip on the gee-gees.

AMY: So, you've helped him out?

JACK: Yeah.

AMY: Why?

JACK just smiles and shrugs again.

DANNY: That's what he did when I asked him.

AMY: Right?…

The three just look at one another.

DANNY: So, what now?

AMY: What do you mean what now? It's your problem.

DANNY: I thought you were helping?

AMY: What gave you that idea?

DANNY: (*Confused.*) Erm…all the help you were giving me.

AMY: You lent it, you get the money.

DANNY: I don't know how.

AMY: And I do?

DANNY: You've got more of a clue than me.

AMY: That bench has got more of a clue than you.

JACK stands, clears his throat.

JACK: If you two are quite finished bickering.

AMY: What?

JACK: I suggest we go to where there's money.

Long pause.

DANNY: London?

AMY: You're a twat.

JACK: I was thinking of town myself. Maybe split up and see how we go on? Many hands make light work and that.

AMY: Why are you getting involved?

JACK: Why are you?

AMY: (*Sighs.*) What time's bus due?

DANNY: (*Waving money.*) Let's get a taxi.

JACK and AMY look at DANNY in disgust.

Bus is fine.

SCENE 13 – CITY CENTRE

JACK, DANNY and AMY have just got off the bus. They are stood outside a pub, 'The Three Legs'. There is a sign advertising a karaoke competition.

JACK: Right then people. It goes like this. Whatever we do today, in the hope of preventing young Danny's crippling, we forgive ourselves for. It's a day off from morality, because needs must when the devil drives, we meet back here at seven. Ok?

AMY nods, DANNY looks confused.

Right then. Good luck.

JACK heads off in one direction, AMY in the other, leaving DANNY.

DANNY: What's the plan? Eh? Jack! (*Beat.*) Amy! What we doing? (*They have gone.*) Tits.

It starts raining.

I fucking hate town.

He looks for a building to enter, goes through a door. As he enters a sign appears above the door. MODERN ART EXHIBITION.

Chapter 2
CONVERSATIONS WITH DEAD PEOPLE

SCENE 14 – TRAIN STATION

AMY is sat crying, a MAN IN A SUIT, pushing a suitcase, stops.

MAN IN SUIT: Excuse me? Is everything ok?

Sobbing, AMY looks up.

AMY: Huh? Oh, yeah it's fine.

MAN IN SUIT: It doesn't seem fine, if you don't mind me saying.

AMY: It's just…it's not your problem, but thanks for taking the time to see if I was alright.

MAN IN SUIT: Do you mind if I sit?

AMY: Feel free.

MAN IN SUIT: (*Long pause.*) Are you sure you're ok?

AMY: Well, I wouldn't say ok. Do you have a tissue?

MAN IN SUIT: I'm sorry, no.

AMY wipes her nose on her sleeve.

AMY: I'm supposed to go to London today.

MAN IN SUIT: Are you?

AMY: I've got an interview, for an air hostess's job, it's what I've always wanted to do.

MAN IN SUIT: Then why are you unhappy?

AMY: My idiot boyfriend carried on with me last night, I've been trying to get rid of him for ages, but he's a bit of an head case, you know? Anyway, he burnt the train ticket, right in front of my face.

MAN IN SUIT is shocked.

So I came here today, hoping to explain to the train misters, but I've got no receipt or proof or owt.

MAN IN SUIT: When's your train?

AMY looks at board.

AMY: Half an hour.

MAN IN SUIT: How much is the ticket?

AMY: Sixty pounds.

MAN IN SUIT thinks for a moment.

MAN IN SUIT: If you get this job, will you leave your boyfriend?

AMY: God yes! I'd be out like a shot.

MAN IN SUIT: So let me lend you it.

AMY: You serious?

MAN IN SUIT: Get the job and you can pay me back, can't you?

AMY: Oh, I will, I really will! I'll give you my name and address and everything. Thank you so much.

MAN IN SUIT passes AMY a pen and paper and gets the money out of his wallet. AMY writes her name and address.

You don't know how much this means to me! Thank you so much.

MAN IN SUIT: It's not a problem.

AMY: But really though, my stepmum always goes on about how there's no gentlemen any more.

AMY hands him back the paper and pen.

But there is, isn't there?

MAN IN SUIT: I suppose there is. I'm glad to help.

AMY: You're a real hero you, you've saved my life here.

MAN IN SUIT is clearly happy with himself. He hands over the £60.

MAN IN SUIT: I'm just doing what's right.

AMY leans over and kisses him.

AMY: (*Intense.*) Thank you.

MAN IN SUIT is on cloud nine but is thrown out by the kiss.

MAN IN SUIT: It's ok. Erm… (*Looks at paper.*) Dorothy. I'm pleased I could help. (*Pause.*) I'd…erm…better get my train.

AMY: Oh yeah, don't you be late. Thank you once again.

MAN IN SUIT: Ok, good luck.

AMY: Fingers crossed.

AMY looks guilty. She takes out a tub of Vicks and smears some underneath her eyes.

SCENE 15 – CASINO, BLACK JACK TABLE

JACK is playing Black Jack.

DEALER: Twenty one.

JACK loses.

Who'd believe it?

JACK: I would.

DEALER starts to shuffle the deck. Enter CATHY, she sits next to JACK.

CATHY: Any luck?

JACK: Yeah, bad.

CATHY puts £20 on the table.

CATHY: (*To DEALER.*) Singles.

Silence while DEALER shuffles.

JACK: Following me?

CATHY: Yeah.

JACK: Bit cloak and dagger?

CATHY: (*Lights a cig.*) Yeah well, I don't fancy turning up at his house without knowing who'll be there and what they'll be doing.

JACK: I won't be there.

CATHY: I'm just making sure.

JACK: (*Pause.*) Why'd you lend him it in the first place?

CATHY: He asked.

JACK: Fairly obvious he couldn't pay it back.

CATHY: If I was that choosy I'd be out of business. (*Beat.*)
They always pay it back. (*Beat.*) Almost always.

JACK: (*Pause.*) Lend me what he owes you and we can both go
home.

CATHY: I take it the cards aren't going your way?

JACK: So, he'll owe me, not you.

CATHY shakes her head.

Why not?

CATHY: I'm not throwing good money after bad. No deal.

DEALER has finished shuffling and gives CATHY her chips.

DEALER: Twenty, single.

CATHY: (*To JACK.*) We gonna play cards then?

SCENE 16 – ART GALLERY

*DANNY is stood, dumbstruck, in the middle of a modern art exhibition.
The words CHAV CULTURE are on a sign. Chav related art pieces are
all around: A portrait of a celebrating footballer in a Burberry kit. A
baby dressed garishly in baseball cap and gold chains. Photographs of
youths in hooded tops transposed onto war torn backgrounds. Collages
of car spoilers and wheel rims. A YOUNG MAN walks around looking
at the pieces giving appreciative cries, he spies DANNY, interestedly.
DANNY looks awkward and confused. Slowly, the YOUNG MAN
edges his way to DANNY, he looks at him as if he was a piece of art.
He nods appreciatively.*

YOUNG MAN: Excellent.

DANNY: Eh?

YOUNG MAN: Do you answer questions?

DANNY: Come again?

The YOUNG MAN doesn't say any more, he stares at DANNY up and down.

YOUNG MAN: It's almost as if, the more people are ostracized, the more they want to display themselves as pariahs. I may not be able to feed and clothe my child but I can afford all this gold. (*Pause.*) It's capitalism in essence. It's beautiful.

DANNY: Beautiful?

YOUNG MAN: Could I touch your cap?

DANNY gives a look to the audience.

SCENE 17 – TRAIN STATION

As before. AMY is crying, CAULDRON sits next to her.

CAULDRON: You ok?

AMY: Yeah, I'm fine… (*Looks up.*)

CAULDRON: I've been watching you, you're good. Good little actress.

AMY: I don't wanna talk to you.

CAULDRON: But we already knew that didn't we?

AMY: Go away.

CAULDRON: I still get e-mails, asking where you are.

AMY: Fuck off Cauldron.

CAULDRON: Where's that little bird gone? Looks like butter wouldn't melt in her mouth.

AMY: I'm not bothered.

CAULDRON: I think they're interested in the pictures where it looks like butter is melting in your mouth though!

AMY: So fucking what? I were dumb enough to let you make a couple of pervy films, it don't mean you've got one over on me Cauldron, it just means you're a scumbag that preys on little girls.

CAULDRON: You made me look a twat today Amy.

AMY: You do alright by yourself mate.

CAULDRON: I'm not here to argue with you.

AMY: I just don't care.

CAULDRON stands.

CAULDRON: Come wi me.

AMY: Yeah right.

CAULDRON: Are you sure you want everyone to know what you're doing? I might shoot it out by accident…Dorothy. Come on, I just wanna talk.

CAULDRON starts walking away. AMY looks around, no way out and he'll find her whenever he wants, she sighs, follows.

SCENE 18 – ART GALLERY

DANNY has YOUNG MAN in a head lock, they are struggling. An ARTIST runs over to break them up.

ARTIST: Leave him!

She breaks them up.

DANNY: Fucking crank!

YOUNG MAN: I thought you were a performer.

DANNY steps forward.

DANNY: What you saying?

ARTIST blocks his path.

ARTIST: He thought you were part of the exhibition.

DANNY: What?

ARTIST: (*To YOUNG MAN.*) I'm very sorry. We're closing now anyhow.

YOUNG MAN looks as if he's about to say something, thinks better of it and leaves, trying to keep his dignity intact. ARTIST turns back to DANNY.

DANNY: I thought performer were some sort of code you know?

ARTIST: It's ok.

DANNY: He touched me cap.

ARTIST: He misunderstood.

DANNY: Right, well…

ARTIST holds her hand out.

ARTIST: I'm Anna, this is my exhibition.

DANNY shakes her hand.

DANNY: It's raining.

ARTIST: Yes, it is.

DANNY looks around him.

DANNY: Is this modern art then?

ARTIST: It's my art.

DANNY thinks, looking around.

DANNY: It looks like mine to be honest.

ARTIST: (*Smiles.*) I take my influence from what I see.

DANNY: Chavs?

ARTIST: Yeah.

DANNY: It's a southerner's word.

ARTIST: What do you call yourself?

DANNY: (*Pointed.*) Danny.

ARTIST: (*Slightly uncomfortable.*) It's more a look at how society treats itself Danny. How culture identifies…

DANNY: Do you make a lot of money out of it?

ARTIST: I get by, but the cliché of the impoverished artist isn't far from the truth. There's eighteen months of work here. Do you smoke?

DANNY: Yeah.

ARTIST: Spliff?

DANNY: Yeah.

ARTIST: Shall we go through to my workshop and smoke one?

DANNY: Why?

ARTIST: I'd like to talk to you.

DANNY: I'm supposed to be doing summat.

ARTIST: Ten minutes. It's really good gear, home grown.

DANNY: (*Eyes light up.*) Aye, why not then!

DANNY cheerfully follows ARTIST.

SCENE 19 – CASINO

JACK and CATHY are playing cards.

DEALER gives CATHY a ten.

DEALER: Bust.

CATHY: Bastard.

Gives JACK a card, he gets a ten.

DEALER: Twenty-one.

CATHY: Spawny bastard!

DEALER deals himself an eight.

DEALER: Seventeen.

DEALER pays JACK.

JACK: I'd have won either way.

JACK picks up his chips.

CATHY: You finished?

JACK: Yeah, always leave when you're up.

CATHY: It's been a pleasure Jack.

DEALER: (*To CATHY.*) You playing again?

CATHY: Do I look like I am?

CATHY stands and intercepts JACK.

In a rush?

JACK: Not particularly.

CATHY indicates the chips.

CATHY: Not enough there, is there?

JACK: It's an improvement.

CATHY: You like a gamble Jack?

JACK: (*Shrugs.*) Steady away.

CATHY: Fancy a chance to double it?

JACK: (*Pause.*) What you thinking?

CATHY indicates they sit down. They do.

CATHY: Ere, did you know in counter terrorism, they train the soldiers to shoot the female terrorists first? The thinking behind it is that the women have had to work harder to get where they are, they're meaner, stronger and more ruthless than the men.

JACK: That Discovery Channel's great, innit?

CATHY: (*Ignores him.*) You knew my uncle Ted didn't you?

JACK: I did, back in the day.

CATHY: I know, I just told you. He reckons you were tasty back then. A man not to be trifled with, he said. What happened?

JACK: I grew up.

CATHY stares at him.

CATHY: I'm being friendly here.

JACK: You mentioned doubling up.

CATHY: I wanna chat first. What happened?

JACK: (*Stands.*) How about I just go?

CATHY: I wanna talk and help you double your money and you just wanna do one.

JACK: (*Smiling.*) Cut the shit, you're trying to play games wi' me is what you're doing, I've been there myself.

CATHY: Ok, no more games, let's have a drink, get some cards and I'll give you your chance.

SCENE 20 – THE CANAL

CAULDRON, walking ahead of AMY, at the canal, CAULDRON stops by the railings. AMY is nervous, she keeps her distance.

AMY: What do you want? I'm busy.

CAULDRON stares at her.

CAULDRON: Come here.

AMY: No, you're all right.

CAULDRON: I'm not gonna do owt, I just wanna talk to you.

AMY: I can hear you.

CAULDRON: (*Laughs.*) Answer for everything.

AMY: Yeah, me dad says that, he likes it though.

CAULDRON: He would.

CAULDRON stares out again.

AMY: Look…

CAULDRON: It was difficult seeing you today.

AMY: What?

CAULDRON: It wasn't nice, seeing you come to rescue that cock.

AMY: His name's Danny.

CAULDRON: I mean, from me of all people.

AMY sighs in frustration.

CAULDRON: Cos, me and you were good together weren't we? We had a laugh.

AMY: Oh yeah it were a right laugh, being used and manipulated.

CAULDRON: I never.

AMY: Yes you did, I was a kid, I was in love and I did whatever you asked.

CAULDRON: So I never forced you.

AMY: You asked me to do them things.

CAULDRON stares out again. Long silence.

CAULDRON: I'm sorry.

AMY: Eh?

CAULDRON: (*Looks her in the eye.*) I'm really, genuinely sorry. I was a cunt.

AMY: (*Thrown out.*) You were.

CAULDRON: I got carried away with the image people had of me. Then somewhere along the line it wasn't pretending and I actually became this animal.

AMY: You used young lasses to get your jollies and make a few quid.

CAULDRON: I did. (*Pause.*) But that's not all I am, is it? The person I was before is still there somewhere. You know me, you know what I can be like.

AMY: Them brief moments between drink and drug binges when you're a human? And why you talking about it as if it's in the past? You still do it.

CAULDRON: I want to change.

AMY: If this is a therapy session Cauldron, go see a professional.

CAULDRON: No. It's you I need to see. (*He moves towards her.*)

AMY: Fuck off!

CAULDRON: (*Stops.*) Don't be like that Amy. I'm asking you for help.

She thinks he's joking and laughs, but when she sees he's serious she stops, suddenly.

AMY: Are you being serious?

CAULDRON: Absolutely. I fucked up with you, big time. I treat (*Pronounced tret.*) you bad Amy, I thought you were just another little tart after me money, but since you left me, I can't stop thinking about you.

AMY: So what you saying?

CAULDRON: I'm saying come back to me.

CAULDRON goes right up to her, she doesn't move away, he puts his hand on her cheek.

I've got enough money now, I can set us up somewhere nice, away from it all. (*Beat.*) What were them dogs you liked?

AMY: Rhodesian Ridgebacks.

CAULDRON: Aye. We'll get a couple of them, big garden for em.

AMY stares at him, she shakes her head.

Why not?

AMY: I don't love you.

CAULDRON: I don't blame you, all I'm asking for is you to give me a chance to prove myself… I love you.

AMY pushes his hand from her cheek and steps back.

AMY: I'm pregnant.

CAULDRON: (*Falters.*) Danny's?

AMY: Yeah.

CAULDRON: You having it?

AMY shakes her head.

CAULDRON: (*Relief.*) Well what's the problem then? Eh? Even if you were gonna keep it, it wouldn't make a difference. I'd love you and I'd love the baby.

AMY looks at him, suddenly shocked.

AMY: Say that again.

CAULDRON: What?

AMY: You'd love me and Danny's baby?

CAULDRON: Course I would.

AMY: You sick bastard!

CAULDRON: What?

AMY: You nearly fucking had me!

CAULDRON: I don't know what you mean.

AMY: Drop it Cauldron. Love Danny's baby? At least keep it realistic.

CAULDRON: Stop being silly lass, what's all this about?

AMY: You just wanna fuck us up, I can't believe you nearly had me.

CAULDRON drops his act and starts laughing.

You twisted bastard!

CAULDRON: It was a step too far wasn't it? I was doing right well till then.

AMY: (*Upset.*) I fucking hate you. You are scum. Beyond help.

CAULDRON: Spit that bile out baby!

AMY: Danny's worth ten of you! I hope you fucking die, I hope you get fucking cancer and die you sick fuck!

Suddenly CAULDRON launches himself at AMY, he hits her two, three times, viciously but calculated. AMY is on the floor. CAULDRON calmly looks around and slowly walks off.

SCENE 21 – ARTIST'S STUDIO

DANNY has a guitar next to him and is smoking a spliff. ARTIST is in another room, making tea. DANNY is spying a mobile phone and camera. He's just about to reach for them…

ARTIST: Sugar?

DANNY: Four please.

ARTIST: (*Pause.*) Sorry?

DANNY: Two…please.

> *DANNY thinks better of nicking the stuff. He enjoys the spliff instead. He reaches for the guitar, but before he gets there, a chord plays. DANNY is stunned. He looks around, suspicious, he looks back at the guitar as it plays again. He nervously and in a girly fashion pushes the guitar away. It plays again, he's proper freaked now. ARTIST enters with two mugs.*

ARTIST: I thought you said four at first.

DANNY: (*Intent on the guitar.*) Nah, that'd be silly.

> *ARTIST puts his drink down, she joins him.*

ARTIST: Surely in this day and age they don't really break your legs?

DANNY: Yeah they do… Anna?

ARTIST: Yeah.

DANNY: I think your guitar's possessed.

ARTIST: Don't be silly!

DANNY: It is! It plays on its own.

ARTIST: Oh… no. (*Calls out.*) Pilly?

> *A guitar answers her.*

Pilly, come and say hello.

DANNY: Who's Pilly?

ARTIST: My partner.

> *Angry guitar.*

(*Quieter.*) My jealous partner, he probably thinks I'm trying to seduce you.

A defiant guitar sound. DANNY looks worried.

Stop being silly darling, come say hello to Danny.

Another defiant guitar sound.

DANNY: Can't he talk?

ARTIST: Of course he can. (*Beat.*) He's a musician.

DANNY: He's not gonna kick off is he?

ARTIST: No, no. He's going through some problems at the moment, he feels he can only communicate through his instrument...

Sad guitar.

He's experimental. Excuse me.

ARTIST stands and goes to find Pilly.

DANNY: He's just fucking mental if you ask me.

SCENE 22 – CASINO

JACK and CATHY are sat, playing cards (Texas Hold em No Limit), with drinks in front of them. CATHY deals out two cards each.

JACK: A fella I used to hang around with got into something in a pub, gave some young un a pasting. It was over a game of pool, the lad was out of order by all accounts. My mate leaves the pub, walks down the road, he's suddenly surrounded by laddo and half a dozen of his friends. (*Beat.*) He gets a machete in his shoulder and seven idiots jumping on his head. Actually stamping on his head. Brown bread before he got put in the ambulance. (*Pause.*) All some people have is a reputation. They're willing to risk everything to keep it. That particular young barm pot is still in Wakey prison. I personally don't believe a rep is worth that, not when any idiot can grab a machete or a baseball bat, or a gun. (*Pause.*) The rules changed. (*Looks at his cards.*)

CATHY: So, you lost your bottle?

JACK: If that's how you want to word it.

CATHY: (*Pause.*) So, it's not because you're ill then?

JACK: (*Surprised.*) Haven't people got owt better to talk about?

CATHY: What you got?

JACK: You tell me.

CATHY: I don't know, that's why I'm asking. (*Beat.*) Summat French isn't it?

JACK: (*Can't help but smile.*) It's name's French… petit mal. I have little blackouts, 'little sleep it means'. (*Beat.*) But it's nowt.

CATHY: Is it gonna kill you?

JACK: No, it's not Cathy, thanks for your concern though. (*Beat.*) I'll raise it ten.

SCENE 23 – ARTIST'S STUDIO

ARTIST returns.

DANNY: Is he cool?

ARTIST: He doesn't want to come through, but you are most welcome Danny.

DANNY: I'd best be off anyhow.

ARTIST: I want to give you something Danny.

DANNY: Do you?

ARTIST: Yes…now I've battled with my conscience here, but Pilly agrees that your need is greater.

She hands DANNY some money.

It's fifteen pounds.

DANNY doesn't know how to react.

DANNY: Cheers.

ARTIST: My crisis was that this money had been collected on behalf of the Haitian workers of the Disney corporation. But I…we feel that 'charity begins at home' is prudent here.

DANNY: Nice one. (*DANNY can't help but grin.*)

ARTIST: Something funny?

DANNY: Nah. (*Stops grinning.*) It's just me… I thought you said Disney.

ARTIST: (*Beat, slightly put out.*) I did.

DANNY: Walt Disney?

ARTIST: Yes. Workers in Haiti are paid the equivalent of fifteen pence an hour. It's a violation of their human rights.

DANNY: (*Pause.*) Like…the *Lion King* and that?

ARTIST: Yes.

DANNY: Right. (*Beat.*) You sure you want me to have it?

ARTIST: You are a victim of capitalism yourself Danny.

DANNY: (*Pocketing the money.*) Oh, I am that, yes…

ARTIST sits next to him. She is staring at him.

I'll never watch *Fantasia* again.

She ignores him.

ARTIST: You have a very caring face Danny.

DANNY: Cheers.

ARTIST: I'd like you to do something for me now.

DANNY looks scared. Pilly's guitar can be heard screeching.

SCENE 24 – CASINO

JACK and CATHY are still playing cards.

CATHY: Bullshit.

JACK: He's not.

CATHY: Course he is!

JACK: If you heard what he's been through…

CATHY: I don't care what you say, he's a loser.

JACK: I'm just saying the boy's had it hard.

CATHY: So's everyone, they've all got sob stories.

JACK: Not like Danny's.

CATHY: (*Changes, suddenly doesn't want this conversation.*) I don't need to hear it.

JACK: Why?

CATHY: I just don't wanna know, I don't care.

JACK: Maybe you do a bit.

CATHY: Believe, I don't.

JACK: Maybe hearing it would make it harder to do what you do.

CATHY: Don't talk daft.

JACK: His mam died when he was a kid.

CATHY: So? My mam's dead, fetch the violins.

JACK: He got put in care a year later.

　　CATHY shrugs.

　　His father had beaten him half to death.

CATHY: Enough now.

JACK: Social took him straight from the hospital.

CATHY: Stop talking.

JACK: Turned out his old man was a twisted bastard.

CATHY: Shut up.

JACK: He used to sell his own son's arse to any man willing to pay…

CATHY: I said shut the fuck up!

　　She looks around, slightly embarrassed, she composes herself.

　　I don't give a fuck.

JACK: Or that's the impression you like to give. Everyone feels compassion Cathy.

CATHY: Not in my family they don't. (*Beat.*) We playing or what?

JACK: It's on you love.

CATHY checks her cards, she's flustered though.

CATHY: You were lying. Just want me to feel sorry for the prick.

JACK: I wish I was lying. (*Beat.*) That kid's dad…dirty bastard.

CATHY shakes it off and focuses on her cards.

You got any kids yourself?

CATHY: No.

JACK: Big family you come from.

CATHY: So?

JACK: So, I'd have thought you'd have kids.

CATHY: If you feel like having one of your little sleeps round about now that'd be fine by me.

JACK: (*Chuckles.*) Sorry I thought you wanted to talk.

CATHY: Yeah, about you, not me. (*Pushes her chips in.*) I'm all in.

JACK: (*Amused.*) Really?

CATHY just stares at JACK, JACK looks at his cards again. Deliberates.

I call.

JACK pushes his chips in. JACK and CATHY turn their cards over.

Fifty-fifty.

CATHY: Aye. By the way Jack, this brave boy who's been through so much. (*Beat.*) He gave me your daughter's name as someone to take on the debt in his absence. (*Pause.*) I think you're backing a loser mate.

CATHY laughs. JACK remains calm. CATHY deals three cards into the table, then another, then another.

Bollox.

SCENE 25 – ARTIST'S STUDIO

DANNY is stood, anxious. ARTIST is out of the room. She re-enters with a digital camera. She starts to set it up.

DANNY: I've…changed my mind.

ARTIST: Please.

DANNY: No, I don't feel comfy, (*Beat.*) I've got to go and get some money anyhow. (*Beat.*) I don't even know what you want me to do.

ARTIST: I want you to be my model.

DANNY: But there's loads of people who'd be better than me, just go to the market, it's full of us.

ARTIST takes a photo, it shocks DANNY.

I weren't even smiling.

ARTIST: I don't want you to smile.

ARTIST takes photo after photo, DANNY protests but then gets into the idea. ARTIST encourages him and soon DANNY is posing for her. She gets him to be more and more aggressive in his poses. His mobile goes. It is AMY. ARTIST continues to photograph him.

DANNY: (*Exhilarated.*) Alright love? How's it going?

AMY: I've been better.

DANNY: What's up? (*Poses.*)

AMY: Nowt…will you come and get me please Danny?

DANNY: (*Suddenly serious.*) Course I will.

ARTIST: That's fantastic…

DANNY holds up his hand to shush ARTIST, ARTIST realises she might have just landed him in it. AMY is silent.

DANNY: Amy?…

AMY: (*Long pause, trying to stay calm.*) What are you doing Danny?

DANNY: Nowt.

AMY: (*Raises her voice.*) While I'm... (*Calm.*) What are you doing?

DANNY: It were raining.

AMY: Who is she?

DANNY: I wouldn't do that to you babe...

AMY: Don't fucking babe me, what's going on?

DANNY: She's just taking some photos.

AMY: (*Lets it all out.*) Yeah? Fucking really?

DANNY: It's not...

AMY: Get her to do a passport photo Danny, cos you can just fuck off! I can't believe I was gonna ask you for help, how thick am I? Danny doesn't do help he just gets it!

DANNY: Amy...

AMY: (*Upset.*) Get to fuck you great big twat. (*She hangs up.*)

DANNY looks at the phone, sees she has hung up, sighs and puts phone away.

ARTIST: I'm sorry, have I got you into trouble?

DANNY: No. (*Pause.*) I'm going to leave now.

ARTIST: (*Holds up camera.*) Just another five minutes?

DANNY: (*Incredulous.*) No. I'm in deep shit here.

ARTIST: Please.

DANNY: No.

ARTIST: Two more minutes?

DANNY: Will you fuck off!!

Silence, a wary guitar sound.

ARTIST: Sorry.

DANNY: Don't be, it's not your fault... I'm sorry.

DANNY gets his things together. Something strange is happening to ARTIST.

ARTIST: Do that again though.

DANNY: What?

ARTIST: Shout at me.

DANNY: Eh?

ARTIST: Shout at me…tell me to fuck off…call me a cunt!

DANNY susses that it is turning her on.

DANNY: Urgh! You sick bitch!

DANNY exits, ARTIST shivers with delight.

Chapter 3
ONCE MORE WITH FEELING

SCENE 26 – ALL

DANNY is stood ringing AMY. AMY is still on the floor, her phone rings, she cuts DANNY off. CATHY is sat in the casino. They sing 'Tender' by Blur.

DANNY and CATHY exit.

JACK enters AMY's space, watches her. They both sing.

SCENE 27 – THE CANAL

JACK looks at AMY just sitting there.

JACK: What happened?

AMY: Not telling you.

JACK: Why not?

AMY: You'd do something silly.

JACK: (*Pause.*) Are you ok though?

AMY: Fine and dandy.

JACK: Your belly?

AMY: I'm getting rid, it'd do me a favour if it was fucked.

JACK: (*Winces.*) Too harsh love.

AMY: (*Apologetic.*) It's fine.

    JACK sits on the floor, next to her.

AMY: That won't do your piles any good.

JACK: My arse, my business.

    They both sit in silence. JACK is staring intently at her.

    Shouldn't we go meet Danny?

AMY: No.

JACK: What's he done?

AMY: Nothing…as usual. We're digging him out of a hole and he's lording it at some bird's house.

More silence. JACK is confused but doesn't ask any more questions. AMY stands, determined.

Come on.

JACK: (*Stands.*) Where?

AMY: Home.

AMY heads off, leaving JACK. JACK doesn't move, he knows his daughter well, she returns. She is torn.

Can we just go home?

JACK: Can we?

AMY is confused, frustrated.

AMY: Sometimes, I wish he would be malicious. I wish he'd shag around or knock me about, because this…this nothing… (*Sighs.*) I left him Dad.

JACK: You did.

AMY: I left him cos I knew I was pregnant and I knew that wouldn't work. He can't look after himself. The boy is useless.

Pause.

JACK: So why are you still stood here?

AMY: (*Exploding, incredulous.*) I don't fucking know! What's wrong with me? You shouldn't see me for dust. (*Beat.*) Why in God's name do I still love him?

JACK comes to comfort her.

JACK: (*Gentle.*) I'll be blowed if I know darling, I can't stand the sight of him myself.

AMY looks up at JACK and laughs.

When you first started seeing him, he came round to see me you know…

AMY: To borrow money?

JACK: No! Divvy. He came round…to ask for my permission to court you.

AMY is dumbstruck.

AMY: Permission to court me? What decade is he in?

JACK: I know… I mean, I appreciated the gesture but I had to put him straight. (*Beat.*) Poor lad was embarrassed, no one had told him, but that's the thing with Danny. (*Beat.*) He's sort of having to make it up as he goes along cos no one sat him down as a nipper and talked to him.

AMY: It's more like having a puppy than a boyfriend.

JACK: You can train a puppy though, can't you?

AMY: (*Pause.*) I wouldn't know, you never let me have one.

JACK: (*Beat.*) Shall we go see how today ends?

AMY nods. They exit.

SCENE 28 – OUTSIDE THE THREE LEGS

DANNY reads the poster advertising a Karaoke contest. The sound of someone singing 'Patience' by Guns n Roses can be heard. DANNY waits, uncertain that AMY will arrive. JACK and AMY enter.

DANNY: (*To AMY.*) I didn't think you'd come.

JACK: (*Hands money to DANNY.*) Two hundred.

DANNY: Thank you Jack.

AMY: (*Does same.*) One-twenty.

DANNY: Oh man! Cheers. Both of you. (*To AMY.*) I wasn't up to owt…

AMY: Whatever.

JACK: How did you get on?

DANNY: I got fifteen.

AMY: Whoop de doo.

DANNY: Plus these.

DANNY pulls out a mobile phone and a digital camera – the ARTIST's.

AMY: Where the hell you rob them from?

JACK: Ah ah!

DANNY: Not even Walt Disney would resent me nicking these. (*Beat.*) We're nearly there…

DANNY hands money and goods over to JACK.

Would you keep hold of it please Jack.

JACK nods and puts money in inside pocket of his jacket.

(*To AMY.*) I'm useless.

AMY: You are.

DANNY: I just didn't know what to do so I went wherever like.

AMY: Nothing new is it?

DANNY: I'm sorry. (*Beat.*) I've put too much on you and your dad's toes. So, with that in mind, I suggest we go in here.

DANNY points to the poster.

AMY: Karaoke?

DANNY: Hundred quid prize.

JACK: Can you sing?

AMY: Yeah, he can.

DANNY: Sort of… I'll give it a go though.

JACK: Let's have it then.

JACK enters pub, AMY goes to follow, DANNY stops her.

DANNY: Amy.

AMY: I don't want to talk Danny.

DANNY: You came back again.

AMY: Under protest.

DANNY: But you still did. Now I know you don't want to be with me no more and that's ok.

AMY: (*Slightly offended.*) Is it?

DANNY: Well, it's not, but it's your choice, you know? I just want to tell you why I borrowed that money.

AMY: (*Shock.*) This should be good.

DANNY: No more bullshit.

AMY: Go on then.

DANNY: (*Steels himself.*) Remember I went to see me dad?

AMY: I found him for you, course I remember.

DANNY: Well I rang him didn't I?

AMY: Then you went to Scarborough to see him.

DANNY pulls a pained expression.

You said he invited you over for the weekend.

Another pained expression.

You made up, he bought you your gold chain.

DANNY: Not quite. He actually told me he'd have me killed if I contacted him again.

Stunned silence.

AMY: So you borrowed the money to pretend to visit him?

DANNY nods.

And you bought that chain yourself?

DANNY nods again.

(*Pause.*) I didn't need you to have a dad.

DANNY: I did.

AMY looks deep into his eyes. She has pity and anger.

AMY: Why didn't you just tell me? That'd have been so much easier.

DANNY: I don't know.

AMY: It's never the easy way is it Danny?

DANNY shrugs.

(*Pause, shakes her head, disappointment.*) Go sing then.

DANNY: Ok.

DANNY enters the pub, AMY follows. CAULDRON walks up, cautiously, so does CATHY. They see one another.

CATHY: Paedophile.

CAULDRON: Fat mental.

CATHY: What you doing here?

CAULDRON: What's it got to do with you Jabba?

CATHY: Ooh, I'd love to kick the fuck out of you.

CAULDRON: (*Smiles.*) But your brothers won't let you.

CATHY: You're a sleazy bastard.

CAULDRON: Give us a kiss.

CATHY: Fuck yourself.

CAULDRON: I nearly can.

CATHY, disgusted, goes to enter.

Ere.

CATHY: What?

CAULDRON: If I give you two hundred will you let me watch?

CATHY: Watch what?

CAULDRON: You breaking his legs.

CATHY: Will I fuck!

CAULDRON: Go on, please!

CATHY: He might pay up, then you'd shit out.

CAULDRON: He won't, I guarantee you of that.

CATHY: (*Confused.*) No.

CATHY enters. CAULDRON barks like a dog after her. Laughing, he sneaks into the pub.

SCENE 29 – INSIDE THE THREE LEGS

Off-stage a cheesy MC is singing Neil Diamond on the karaoke, JACK and AMY are sat at a table. DANNY joins them.

DANNY: (*Shouting.*) Shall we get a drink?

JACK hands DANNY a tenner.

JACK: Don't spend it all!

AMY: Get some crisps.

DANNY: What do you fancy Jack?

JACK: Bitter.

DANNY heads off to the bar, the MC comes to the end of the song with a dramatic flourish.

MC: (*Voice off.*) Thank you, thank you. Remember tonight's competition is open to everyone but you have to submit your slips a s a p. Slips and songbooks can be found on the tables. (*Sincere.*) Hey. Good luck.

A song comes on, quietly, 'You Got the Love' by The Source featuring Candi Staton. AMY starts to write out a slip. JACK observes.

JACK: Does he know it?

AMY: No, I'm deliberately picking a song he's never heard of so he gets his legs broke.

JACK: Little madam.

AMY: Fat lad. (*Pause, stops writing.*) Here's a question.

JACK: What?

AMY: After all his dad's done to him, why does he listen to the same music?

JACK thinks. Shrugs.

It's kinda weird?

JACK: I couldn't pretend to understand.

DANNY comes back with drinks.

DANNY: Here we go.

DANNY sits and hands out the drinks. They drink in silence. DANNY raises his glass.

To my legs!

AMY and JACK smile.

AMY / JACK: To Danny's legs.

AMY: Here.

Hands DANNY the slip.

DANNY: Don't I even get to choose my own song?

DANNY reads it.

You sure?

AMY nods.

Fairy snuff, good choice. (*Beat.*) I'm sorry.

AMY: It's ok, I shouldn't have got angry, it's not your fault your dad's a cunt.

JACK: Oi!

AMY: Sorry…

JACK: That man is a fucking cunt and don't you ever forget it.

DANNY: I'll drink to that.

They all drink.

AMY: I'm just off to the loo.

DANNY: You ok?

AMY: Yeah, it's perfectly normal.

AMY sets off to the toilet. JACK turns to DANNY.

DANNY: She's done that a lot today.

JACK: What's that?

DANNY: Amy's been looking pale and rushing off to the toilet a lot.

JACK: Right.

DANNY: You don't think…

JACK: (*Nervous.*) What?

DANNY: You don't think she's got food poisoning or summat?

JACK laughs.

What?

JACK: Nothing lad.

They both sit in silence.

Future reference Daniel.

DANNY leans in.

DANNY: What's that?

JACK: If you need a guarantor…you put my name, not hers.

DANNY: (*Sheepish.*) Sorry about that.

JACK: It's ok. (*Beat.*) Thank you for not doing a runner.

DANNY: It never crossed my mind Jack.

JACK smiles, he lovingly slaps DANNY's face.

JACK: Go hand that in Danny.

DANNY takes the slip to the MC, JACK drinks.

SCENE 30 – TOILETS AT PUB

AMY is throwing up in the sink, CATHY enters, she notices AMY.

CATHY: Too much to drink lass?

AMY: (*Between retching.*) No. Can you hold my hair back please?

CATHY looks around, reluctantly holds AMY's hair back.

Why is there no toilet doors?

CATHY: They must get a lot of smackheads in. You sure you aint pissed?

AMY: Positive. I thought morning sickness did what it says on the tin.

CATHY: You pregnant?

AMY: Yeah. (*Breaths out.*) I'm done I think.

CATHY lets her hair go, AMY stands.

Thanks for that.

CATHY: S'alright. How far gone are you?

AMY: Two months. Have I got any on me?

CATHY looks.

CATHY: No, you're clear.

AMY picks up her bottle of beer.

You shouldn't be drinking you know.

AMY: It's not a problem.

CATHY: I didn't think you were supposed to.

AMY: (*Sad.*) You're not. (*Pause.*) Thanks for your help though.

CATHY: Ere! You ok?

AMY: Yeah I'm fine.

AMY goes to leave.

CATHY: Are you sure about it?

AMY stops.

AMY: About what?

CATHY: None of my business like, but you might regret it later.

AMY: I can't think like that.

CATHY: It happens though.

AMY: I know. (*Beat.*) No offense like, because you are frigging huge, but are you one of them religious types? Pro-life and that?

CATHY: No, am I bollocks! It's just…there's some that would give owt to be in your shoes.

AMY: Please don't.

CATHY: You could adopt.

AMY: I feel bad enough as it is, please.

CATHY: Just speaking me mind.

AMY: Yeah. Thanks.

AMY exits.

CATHY: Fucking slut.

SCENE 31 – INSIDE PUB

AMY re-enters, joins JACK and DANNY. Someone is enthusiastically singing the end of 'Beautiful' by Christina Aguilera.

DANNY: You ok?

AMY: I'm fine Danny.

DANNY: Just you took a while.

AMY: I had a shit if you must know.

JACK looks disgusted.

DANNY: I'm on next.

AMY: (*With a sigh.*) Go for it Danny.

DANNY: I need a shit now.

JACK: Can we not, please.

DANNY: Sorry Jack.

They wait. DANNY is staring at AMY.

AMY: What?

DANNY: I don't want you to leave me.

AMY: We'll talk about it tomorrow Danny. You've got more important things to worry about.

DANNY: There's nothing more important.

MC: Thank you, that was…Christina Agweralera, ably sung by the lovely Maggie. Can we have Danny Wilde up next please?

DANNY: Oh, shitty death.

JACK: Go on son, do your best.

DANNY: I can't move.

AMY: Get up div.

DANNY: I can't move!

JACK reaches over and tweaks his nipple. DANNY yelps and jumps up.

JACK: There we go.

DANNY: Cheers.

DANNY goes to the stage. AMY and JACK clap him.

AMY: Come on Danny!

JACK: Sing for your supper lad!

JACK looks at AMY. He smiles.

AMY: Shut up fat man.

DANNY is on stage, he nervously takes the mic. Music starts, 'Lately' by Stevie Wonder.

He starts singing, quite nervously, but as the song goes on he gets much better, DANNY believes. AMY is transfixed, JACK looks at her and smiles. We see CATHY and CAULDRON, on either side, CATHY watches, impressed, CAULDRON makes puking actions and the wanker sign. JACK sees CATHY, he walks up to her, without her noticing, he rubs her back, at first she doesn't respond and welcomes the touch. Then she realizes, pushes JACK away and points an accusing finger; JACK, laughing, backs off. There is something tender about this. JACK returns to AMY. He and AMY hold hands (AMY initiates this). Song ends, AMY and JACK stand and applaud him. Beaming, DANNY returns to the table, to back-slapping from JACK. DANNY and AMY face each other. AMY takes DANNY's hand and starts to drag him outside. Music comes on ('Love Cats' by the Cure) AMY stops, goes back to JACK.

AMY: I'm not doing this for you.

JACK: Heaven forbid! (*Serious.*) Amy.

AMY: What?

JACK: If you're not keeping the baby, don't ever tell him.

AMY: I won't. (*Beat.*) I need some more time yet.

JACK: That's good.

AMY: So… I was wondering if I could…

JACK: Of course you can I'm bloody sick of that caravan.

AMY goes outside with DANNY. JACK is alone, drinking, shakes his head. CAULDRON sits opposite him.

Cauldron.

CAULDRON: Jacky.

JACK: What you doing?

CAULDRON: Nothing.

JACK: Then do it somewhere else please.

CAULDRON: (*Camp voice.*) He's got a right lovely voice your son-in-law.

JACK: He has. Once again, what you doing?

CAULDRON: Waiting.

JACK: For what?

CAULDRON: You.

JACK: My dance card's full. You'll have to get in early next time.

CAULDRON: So, you helped him get the money then?

JACK: Did you see Amy earlier?

CAULDRON: I don't know what you mean. (*Pause.*) You wouldn't have done that for me would you?

JACK: No, I wouldn't.

CAULDRON: Yet you'd do it for that scruffy bastard? You never liked me did you Jack?

JACK: (*Long pause.*) What's to like?

SCENE 32 – OUTSIDE THREE LEGS

DANNY and AMY. AMY hands DANNY the £200 her dad gave her for the clinic.

DANNY: What's this?

AMY: Some money I had in the bank.

DANNY: You want me to have it?

AMY: That's sort of the point of today isn't it? Money.

DANNY: You serious?

AMY: Yes.

DANNY: We've done it then!

AMY: I know.

DANNY: Thank you. (*He hugs her, she doesn't respond.*)

AMY: I've got some things I need to think about Danny so I think I will stay at me mam and dad's.

DANNY: (*Deflated.*) Yeah.

AMY: But I'd like to…maybe like isn't the right word. I stupidly want to keep seeing you.

DANNY: Serious?

AMY: Serious.

Awkward moment. DANNY looks like he's going to cry.

You gonna fucking kiss me then or what?

DANNY: Yeah course.

They kiss.

SCENE 33 – INSIDE PUB

CAULDRON: I don't have kids so I don't know. But, if you have a daughter, does it torture you? The thought of her getting fucked? Some dude getting stuck in? Her face like a plasterer's radio? 'Harder, harder, hurt me!' (*Laughs.*) Does it?

Pause. JACK stares at him.

Wanna go for me Jack? Getting stressed?

JACK: I do have a certain urge…

JACK feels strange, tries to shake it off.

CAULDRON: Not planning on having one of your blackout thingies are you?

JACK: Go away.

CAULDRON: She made films you know, I can make you a copy if you're interested, there's not much storyline but the climax is good.

JACK zones out. CAULDRON checks.

Now that's what I was waiting for.

CAULDRON reaches into JACK's jacket and takes the money, phone and camera. He slaps JACK round the face.

That's for even considering it.

CATHY comes over to him.

CATHY: What the fuck are you doing?

CAULDRON: Bit of business fat lass. Stay out.

CATHY stands in front of CAULDRON.

CATHY: No.

CAULDRON: What do you care? You get to bust up Danny now. (*Pause.*) Unless you got a soft spot for old Jack have you?

CATHY: Don't take it.

CAULDRON: Already have. Now shift it, I know it might take a while.

CATHY: No.

CAULDRON: Move.

CAULDRON thinks about pushing past.

CATHY: You know I'd kill you if you tried it.

Stand off.

CAULDRON: Your brothers won't be happy, and your old man? If he knew you'd gone soft. Can't ruin the Whites' reputation can you?

CATHY: Biggest mistake they ever made was working with you.

CAULDRON: It's not work babe, it's pleasure. And they do, so tough shit. (*Beat.*) Move your fat arse.

CATHY thinks, steps aside and CAULDRON exits. CATHY looks at JACK, regretful, then exits.

SCENE 34 – OUTSIDE THREE LEGS

AMY and DANNY are cuddling.

DANNY: I wouldn't have blamed you if you'd have left for good.

AMY: I can't leave you Danny, you're like bloody heroin.

DANNY: Addictive?

AMY: No, no matter how much harm you know it's doing you, you can't turn your back on it.

DANNY: (*Thinks.*) It's better than nowt.

CAULDRON enters.

CAULDRON: Awww. Ain't it sweet.

AMY and DANNY part, AMY is scared.

DANNY: Fuck off.

CAULDRON: Gladly. (*Blows a kiss to AMY.*) See you again Amy darling.

CAULDRON exits.

DANNY: Why didn't he batter me?

AMY doesn't reply.

Are you ok?

She nods.

AMY: I hate him.

DANNY: What was he doing here?

AMY: I dunno.

DANNY: (*Sudden realisation.*) Your dad!

AMY understands, they both run into the pub.

SCENE 35 – INSIDE PUB

JACK is raging, smashing up the place, like a madman. AMY rushes over to him and calms him down.

AMY: Dad!

JACK: He took everything.

AMY: We know.

JACK: That piece of fucking garbage is dead!

AMY: Dad calm it, you'll get us kicked out.

JACK: I know I promised you and your mam, I know I did, but that man is getting it!

AMY: Please Dad, you're scaring me.

DANNY: It's alright Jack.

JACK: No it's not, he's taken the money!

DANNY: Jack, it's alright!

JACK: He took your money lad, are you deaf? What you give it to this old man for eh?

DANNY: Balls to the money, it was never meant to happen.

JACK: What are you on about? They're gonna break your legs kid! And it's my fault.

DANNY laughs.

(*To AMY.*) What did you do to him outside?

DANNY: Jack, I'd have never got that money on me own. I'm no worse off am I? It's no one's fault but me own. I borrowed it. I'll pay up.

JACK: I'll come with you. I can talk her out of it.

DANNY: No.

AMY: Danny…

DANNY: I said no.

JACK: Go to my house for tonight, I'll get the money for you tomorrow.

DANNY: No. I'm going home.

AMY: There's ways around this Danny.

DANNY: And this is what I'm doing. I can't hide from it. (*To JACK.*) I want to thank you for helping me.

DANNY shakes JACK's hand.

JACK: I feel terrible lad.

DANNY: Don't. You've done more for me today than my own dad's ever done. I'm happy.

DANNY turns to leave. AMY follows him.

What you doing? This is the coolest exit I've ever made in my life!

AMY: Coming with you.

DANNY: No you're not.

AMY: Oi! You might be all Bruce Willis at the moment but that's my flat as well as yours. I'm coming, end of.

DANNY: (*To JACK.*) Tell her Jack.

JACK: I've been telling her for seventeen years mate. It's your turn.

DANNY: You gonna watch her break my legs?

AMY: If it comes to it.

DANNY: You can deal with that?

AMY: If you can. Look on the bright side, I'll be able to get you to hospital.

DANNY: Don't have any choice do I?

AMY: You never have had.

DANNY and AMY exit. JACK starts to put the pub back in order.

Chapter Four
THE GIFT

SCENE 36 – DANNY AND AMY'S FLAT

DANNY and AMY are waiting. DANNY is pacing around, AMY's watching him.

AMY: You ok?

DANNY: No. I should've got a bottle of gin.

AMY: Maybe she'll be happy with two hundred.

DANNY: Maybe I'll get a job at Harvey Nicks.

AMY stands.

AMY: Fuck this.

DANNY: What?

AMY: Let's go.

DANNY: Where?

AMY: Do a runner. I've got a cousin in Dewsbury.

DANNY: We've got two hundred quid to our name…and your family's here.

AMY: I can't watch them break your legs.

DANNY: We're out of choices love.

DANNY cuddles her. They sit.

AMY: I don't want you to get hurt.

DANNY: Good.

DANNY smiles at her.

AMY: What you smiling for? You big, gormless bastard!

Enter CATHY. With baseball bat.

CATHY: Right piss flap, time's up.

AMY: Fucking hell it's you!

CATHY: (*To AMY.*) Aye.

AMY: You knew I was with Danny?

CATHY: Yeah, so what?

DANNY: What she on about?

AMY: We met.

CATHY: (*To DANNY.*) Right then! Business.

DANNY: I haven't got it.

CATHY: Eh?

DANNY: I haven't got it Cathy. I've got two hundred.

CATHY: (*Drops her head, she seems to be contemplating.*) Ok.

> *CATHY props the baseball bat against the wall. She takes her coat off and picks it up again.*

DANNY: I take it that won't do?

CATHY: All or nothing.

AMY: Danny.

DANNY: Can I have more time Cathy…please?

CATHY: No.

DANNY: I can get it.

CATHY: It's too late. Stand up.

> *DANNY can't move.*

> I said fucking stand up!

DANNY: I can't, me legs are shaking.

CATHY: (*Through teeth.*) Stand up.

AMY: This is stupid, what's breaking his legs gonna do?

CATHY: It projects the correct company image. Last chance or I'll swing for your head.

> *Slowly, DANNY does. CATHY swings back.*

AMY: I'll give you my baby!

CATHY: What?

DANNY: What!?

AMY: Just let him off, I'll have it and I'll give it to you.

DANNY: Amy, what you talking about?

AMY holds a silencing hand up to DANNY.

AMY: It's what you want isn't it?

CATHY doesn't reply.

So, here you go. I'm making you an offer.

DANNY: Are you pregnant?

AMY: (*Blunt.*) Yeah.

CATHY: (*Soft, almost defeated.*) Don't fuck with me.

AMY: What?

CATHY: Don't say it if you don't mean it.

AMY: Ere, you know yourself what I were gonna do, I told you. Just don't do Danny and it's yours.

DANNY: A baby?

AMY: Be quiet Danny.

CATHY: You swear?

AMY: I swear. I'll put it in writing, I'll sign owt.

CATHY: (*Almost in tears.*) I'd look after it, real good.

AMY: I hope you will. Do we have a deal?

CATHY drops the baseball bat.

CATHY: Yeah. Yeah we have a deal. Fucking hell yes.

AMY: Right, good then.

AMY gets her cigarettes out of her pocket and throws them to CATHY.

I'd better quit, hadn't I?

CATHY: Yeah you had, and no more drinking from now on.

AMY: Ok.

CATHY: You'd do this for me?

AMY: I'm doing this for Danny.

DANNY: I fucking love you.

AMY: I know you do.

DANNY leans over and gives her a gentle kiss.

DANNY: Now it's my turn to prove it.

AMY starts to speak, but DANNY puts his finger over her mouth.

My turn.

DANNY picks up the baseball bat and hands it to CATHY.

CATHY: What?

DANNY: I'm not giving up my kid to you.

CATHY: She said…

DANNY: I don't give a fuck, cos that's my baby n all and I choose not to give it to you.

CATHY: Don't you dare take this away from me!

AMY: Danny it's not your decision!

DANNY: Yes it is. Cos it's my legs that you two are dealing over and I say, fuck it, break em, cos that child is mine.

AMY: Danny.

DANNY: My choice Amy.

DANNY stands in front of CATHY and opens his arms.

Get it done then.

CATHY: Don't.

AMY: You want this baby?

CATHY is confused and stands with baseball bat.

DANNY: Course I do. I want it more than anything, well… I never knew I did, but I know now.

CATHY: (*To AMY.*) I'll pay you.

DANNY: No.

CATHY: (*To DANNY.*) Five grand.

DANNY: Could be fifty, I don't care.

CATHY: You can't bring a baby up.

DANNY: Yes I can. I'll get a job. Any old job, I don't mind.

AMY: You've said yourself it's not right bringing up a baby in all of this.

DANNY: Then we'll get out of this, together. I mean it.

AMY: (*Smiles.*) I know you do.

DANNY: Hurry up then, I'm shitting myself.

DANNY shuts his eyes. CATHY stares at AMY.

AMY: It's his baby Cathy. Sorry though, it must be shit, not being able to have kids.

CATHY looks back at DANNY.

CATHY: It is.

Long pause. CATHY raises the baseball bat.

AMY: Godmother?

DANNY opens one eye.

CATHY: Eh?

AMY: You can be godmother. (*Beat.*) Danny?

DANNY: It's fine by me. (*To CATHY.*) You'd be hell of a godmother to have.

AMY: Yeah.

CATHY: What would it entail?

AMY: Babysitting'd come in useful, we'll do it proper, christening and that, you'd be there for it when it needs you.

Long pause as CATHY considers.

CATHY: It's fuck all compared to what you were offering.

AMY: I know.

CATHY: So why should I take it?

AMY: I don't know.

DANNY: For what it's worth, I think you should take it.

CATHY stares at DANNY.

What?

CATHY continues staring.

Cathy?

CATHY: Jack said you weren't a waster.

DANNY: (*Chuffed.*) Did he?

CATHY: He annoys me does Jack.

DANNY: Aye…well?

CATHY: (*Pause, slowly nods.*) We're done. (*Lowers baseball bat.*)

DANNY: We are?

CATHY: Debt free.

AMY: Thank you Cathy.

DANNY moves away, with wobbly legs.

DANNY: Thank fuck for that!

DANNY rubs his legs.

Did you hear that boys!?

AMY comes to hug DANNY.

Why didn't you tell me you were pregnant?

AMY: Shhh.

They remain in a hug.

CATHY: Erm… I'm worth it.

AMY: Worth what?

CATHY: I'm not all bad.

AMY: No-one is. (*Pause.*) Do you want to come to the doctors with me tomorrow?

CATHY: Yeah.

AMY: Meet you here? About ten?

CATHY: (*Nods.*) Right, tomorrow then.

CATHY turns to leave.

DANNY: Cathy? (*She stops and turns.*) Can I have my chain back? Please…

CATHY stares at him, she looks softer, a gentler character. She walks up to DANNY, smiling. Suddenly she cuffs him round the head.

CATHY: Don't take the piss.

CATHY exits.

AMY: What do you want with that chain?

DANNY: Family heirloom. (*Beat.*) Give us a kiss gorgeous.

AMY: I'm having a baby, I can't do any strenuous movements.

DANNY: So, I'm gonna have to do everything for the next nine months?

AMY: Yes.

DANNY: Good.

He kisses her.

AMY: Dad'll be happy.

They cuddle.

EPILOGUE
SCENE 37 – CAULDRON'S FLAT

CAULDRON's flat, in darkness. CAULDRON enters. He potters about in the dark and then turns a light on, he sits on the sofa. JACK stands up behind him, with a baseball bat, CATHY stands up next to JACK, again with baseball bat. They nod at one another.

JACK: Now then.

END